SAVING OUR CHILDREN

AN IN-DEPTH LOOK AT GUN VIOLENCE IN OUR NATION AND OUR SCHOOLS

BY

DANIEL FRIEDMAN

Bloomington, IN  Milton Keynes, UK

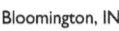

AuthorHouse™
1663 Liberty Drive,
Suite 200
Bloomington, IN 47403
www.authorhouse.com
Phone: 1-800-839-8640

AuthorHouse™ UK Ltd.
500 Avebury Boulevard
Central Milton
Keynes, MK9 2BE
www.authorhouse.co.uk
Phone: 08001974150

This book is a work of non-fiction. Unless otherwise noted, the author and the publisher make no explicit guarantees as to the accuracy of the information contained in this book and in some cases, names of people and places have been altered to protect their privacy.

First published by AuthorHouse 8/8/2006

ISBN: 1-4259-3957-0 (sc)

Library of Congress Control Number: 2006904497

Printed in the United States of America
Bloomington, Indiana

This book is printed on acid-free paper.

<u>DEDICATION</u>

I dedicate this book to my family, my community,
my teachers, and to all those who lost their
lives to gun violence in our schools.

"A journey of a thousand miles
must begin with a single step."

-Lao-Tzu,
   The Way of Lao-Tzu

CONTENTS

The author of this poem was a Junior in Columbine High School and was in the choir room when the shootings began.

<u>11:21 A.M.</u>

I lie on my bed
numb,
unemotional,
non-feeling.
Fear stains my memories as I reflect
on a placid morning in Littleton.
A usual day in choir
We prepare for concerts,
blithely indulging in normal routine.
Carefree...Content...
Unaware...

A sudden blast startles us.
A chemistry explosion?
Deafening eruptions penetrate "Ave Maria."
Sinuous voices now punctuated by gunshots,
the demonic splintering the angelic.

The choir hushes
to the rhythm of pounding hearts.
Students scream though halls
as terror burns itself on innocent faces.

Tick, Tick, Tick - 11:21 -
lives are forever changed.
Shock...Hysteria...

Why?
The sound of bombs ignite horror through our veins
and send chills
that pinch the skin like needles.

Some run.
Some stand paralyzed in shock,
numbness engulfing all other emotions.
Billows of powder now blanket the hall,
creating ghostly images.
I look though the delicate webs of cotton
and see the fruits of hatred.

Bullets shatter glass
and invade bodies,
as malice sears the souls of the perpetrators.

A student prays;
another hides in stunned confusion;
a teacher bleeds.

Like children
we are helpless,
longing to be in mama's arms .
Screaming...Frantic...
Why?

Two faces
are plastered against the window.
The horror in their eyes strips away
my consciousness.
My first instinct is to run;
I duck as bullets spray the halls.

Our school is now the grounds of warfare -
moral fighting
in a field of bombs and bullets.
Weapons that have fallen into the wrong hands
have only one purpose and they
are killing us and all I hear is gunfire.
Crackling, Crackling,
Humming, bursting, screaming, ringing, what now,
Too much
Too soon
Too young
So scared
Help us.

I struggle to escape but am slowed
as if trudging though water.
Through the front doors I see milky clouds
that absorb the sun;
I see the golden light and sunburned pavement.
I cannot get there fast enough.

I am almost to the door.
A bullet ricochets off the pane.
The glass swirls like a droplet on water,
creating rings that shiver and spread,
shattering as I dash though the door -
All is silent.
I have escaped hell.

There is a dark room
where ten broken bodies lie,
and where others play dead.
In the darkness of the library,

angels embrace the lifeless,
and their wings flicker light
against the wall of helpless shadows.
God now wraps His arms
around the school
and gathers the souls of the lost,
makes strong the souls of the weak,
cries for the violence on Earth.

Time picks up and I am vulnerable, insecure.
A dog's bark screams like bullets.
Who to trust?
Our haven is destroyed,
and we are scattered.

I sit immobilized,
while anxiety and guilt wrap themselves around me
and consume me.
Angry...Numb...
Why?
Are there answers in silence...?
Because I am asking you and you don't answer...

Or maybe the silence is just you listening.

- Joanna Gates

Reprinted With Permission.

INTRODUCTION

Every day in America, our many leaders on the federal, state, and local levels of government, debate numerous issues and determine the law accordingly. Among these issues are health care, tax rates, Social Security, environmental protection, and many other important matters. They also discuss many policies that would better the condition of Americans nationwide.

However, amid all the deliberations of many issues, there is something that is rarely discussed. Solving this issue would improve the lives of all Americans, and that is the issue of gun control. We can no longer continue to view this issue with the smug complacency that has been the trademark of our past approaches. It is the responsibility of our leaders to act on this issue, and act now. These leaders are elected by the people who have been pained by the inaction of our government to help them in this matter.

Let there be no doubt; the purpose of this book is not to try to bring an end to the use of guns entirely. I do not support that reform in any way. The reform that I am proposing is to limit the use, access, and availability of guns around this country. The main purpose of this book is to bring the current situation to the attention of all Americans. This problem is in no way limited to a certain group of people. This problem is hurting all Americans, putting lives at risk every day, and making America a more dangerous place to live.

In 1776, our Founding Fathers fought a war that would forever change the history of the world. They were tired with their current system of government. They were tired of oppression and hardships, and having their basic civil liberties denied. As a result, they formed a group of people who shared their desire for freedom, and an interest in the formation of a new country; free of harsh rule, despotism, and misery.

They fought a war, and people died. Not just a few people, but hundreds, thousands, died. They died for the things they believed in. They died knowing that their dream would one day come to pass; that their children would live in a land that was free, and live in any manner they wished.

On a hot summer day, a man named Thomas Jefferson drafted on a piece of paper, words that will never be forgotten: "We hold these truths to be self-evident, that all men are created equal, that they are endowed by their Creator with certain unalienable Rights, that among these are Life, Liberty, and the pursuit of Happiness."

These words changed the lives of millions of people. It gave hope to so many, and granted freedom to all. The words of the Declaration of Independence still echo throughout this country every day, and its meaning still lives on in every American's heart and soul, in all their actions and words.

The Founding Fathers fought a war for Independence. Yet now, once again, we are fighting another war. This war is the fight of all Americans to win their independence over the dangers of reckless firearm use. Not to eliminate all firearms, but to keep them out of the hands of children and would-be criminals. That is a war that I, and others, will never stop fighting- not until we win.

Every day, in your neighborhood, and across America, millions of children board the bus to go to school. Some are boys, some are girls; some are white, some are black; some are natural born citizens, and some are not. Yet they are all united by the common title of American. No single group of people is more or less susceptible to the effects of gun violence; all demographics have the same chance of being victimized.

Some students go to school, and live in constant fear of others every day of their lives. These "others" that I refer to are not criminals or murderers, these others are the classmates of those who go to school every day with trepidation. These classmates bring weapons to school- guns, knives, and other deadly weapons.

We have seen on television the destruction of the lives of helpless, innocent children. Some of these children are athletes, some are gifted, some are active in their school or community, and some stay for after school activities. These children are between the ages of five and nineteen. These are young minds, with a future lying before them. These are the children who will someday be our leaders, our teachers, and our businessmen and women.

These children have a bright and successful future ahead of them, yet they go to school every day, and many of them wonder if it will be their last.

These children are our future. These children deserve to have the right to go to school without fear or concern for their lives and safety. Yet every day, these children are being senselessly attacked, sometimes fatally, and some at point blank range. This epidemic destruction of our children needs to be stopped immediately.

Consider if you will, the mind of a fourteen-year-old boy, right before he is to be killed without reason. What is he thinking the moment before his life is done? What is he thinking when his dreams and future disappear? He is an innocent child who has done nothing wrong, yet he is to be shot by someone who has killed before. The bodies lying in the hallways and classrooms of the school are witness to his murderers' readiness to kill. He has destroyed lives before, with no justification for those slayings, and now this fourteen-year-old child crouching under his desk will be the next to die. He will be killed, not by the hands of an adult, but by the hands of another fourteen-year-old boy who has lost sight of his own future.

The fourteen-year-old boy is not the only one who suffers, for he has a family as well. He has a father, a mother, brothers and sisters. He has grandparents, aunts, uncles, and cousins. All of them will suffer, as they deal with the loss of their young one. They are one with the actual victim, and a part of them is shot dead along with the fourteen-year-old.

Along with the victim's family, the school and the community mourn as well, for they have lost a student, a friend, a neighbor. Every day thereafter, instead of having 27 students in a classroom, there will only be 26. An empty chair and desk are the only indication that someone isn't there anymore. But in the hearts of all the classmates, there is a longing to see and to speak with the dead, the murdered, and the innocent.

It is time for America to stand up against the assault on the student body and their communities. It is time to act now, for if we don't, another murder will take place, another child will fall, and another town will suffer. If action isn't taken, more children will die. We may be held responsible for the killing of a great hero, or a child who was destined to become the President of the United States. If we ignore this problem, then we may be responsible for the murder of our own friend, neighbor, relative, or even our own child.

Although I have a strong sense of love of country, and believe that most things in America are good and well, and the way it ought to be, this problem is one thing that truly ought not to be. This is the murder of people in our families, our communities, and in our country. These people who have been killed by firearms are not just brothers and sisters, or fathers and mothers; they are also Americans. Rather than hide in shame, and look past the sad fact that is the current presence of gun violence in our communities, as an American who is proud of his country, I am making a plea for vigorous reform. What has once been a minor problem is now a calamity that begs for action. Our country is in need of help, and the people of America need it now.

The focus of this work, and what the gun control movement should be about, is on the prevention of gun crimes committed by young people in America. If we are to be successful in creating a safer America, our concern must be with those who will lay the groundwork for the future. By concerning ourselves with youth violence and weapons abuse by young people, we will be able to ensure a more significant victory in the long-term battle to make our communities safer.

We cannot go on and say that we should not be held responsible for the murders that occur because of our own ignorance. Now is the time to act. Now is the time to take charge of this problem. Now is the time, before another child becomes a statistic. Before we turn on the news at night, and learn of another school shooting.

We must act swiftly and rationally, before it is too late. Now we have the resources, now we have the means, and now we have more of a reason to act. It is important for every person to do their part, and give their fair share of support to new gun control laws. We must create reform without compromise, laws without loopholes, and lives without fear. While this may be hard to accomplish, it is not harder than seeing another teenager succumb to a bullet fired by a classmate who is jealous, angry, or without aim. We must take aim, and help in every conceivable way. We cannot control who goes to school every day, but we can control what goes on in our children's schools. We can, and we must.

Daniel Friedman

March 2006

PART I:

THE GUN CULTURE

EARLY HISTORY OF THE GLOBAL GUN CULTURE

Since the beginning of time, mankind has been fascinated with weapons. From the nomads to the hunter-gatherers, and onward to civilization and today, weapons have served many purposes. The most important among them has been the survival of mankind, the practical uses of which can be further broken down to the arts of self-defense as well as war. Before humans were even able to speak, they used weapons to kill animals, and on occasion other humans, just to survive. As civilization began to take hold across the world, each group of people developed and perfected their own weapons. Asians developed samurai swords, and Native Americans used bows and arrows. Europeans had guns centuries later, which required the use of ammunition, namely gunpowder, which had previously been developed by the Chinese.

Upon closer examination, the nature and history of all these weapons can be found by the details of their physical structure. By looking at that, we can tell much about their use and the mindset of those who created them.

Throughout history, weapons have been predominantly used by males, young and old, and have always been associated with men and virility.

It was in the middle of the 14ᵗʰ Century that Europeans began to develop portable weapons. They were called hand cannons or fire sticks. As time passed, improvements were made to these weapons, and their availability increased. Some European nations, frightened by the prospects of the death and destruction that might follow as a result of the mass production of these weapons, tried with some initial success, to limit their access. As intercontinental travel began, these weapons were shipped overseas, en masse.

Political leaders and philosophers of the time differed in their approach to these new weapons. Philosophers believed that if the citizenry gathered up arms, it might compel their governments to become more democratic. Kings, such as England's Henry VIII, feared chaos. Strict rules were enforced, which forbade almost anyone from even owning a gun. Over time, even the carrying of such weapons made one liable for the death penalty.

In 1651, Thomas Hobbes published "Leviathan", which said that the monarchs have the absolute right to maintain arsenals to control the people. This was in line with the writings of Jean Bodin, who in the early 1600's wrote that monarchs had to preserve their power. To do this, he said, it was necessary to disarm the citizenry. However, when Hobbes wrote his work later on, he also argued that each citizen had to be responsible for their personal safety against criminals and tyrannical leaders.

In 1686, John Locke published his famous "Two Treatises on Government", which was used and quoted often by the

Founding Fathers when they prepared the Declaration of Independence and the Constitution. Locke reasoned that a social contract between the government and the governed was necessary, and that the people had the right to revolt if their human rights were being violated. Therefore, all citizens had the right to defend themselves from such a possibility by any means available, including the possession of arms.

In the 17th Century, England passed many laws to raise the requirements for gun ownership. At first, they only allowed the nobility to own guns, but also required that the annual salary of a prospective gun owner had to exceed 100 pounds, an outrageous amount at the time. In 1670, Parliament raised that figure to 150 pounds. As the use and popularity of guns grew among the nobility, the government kept trying to restrict its use more and more, so that only the extremely wealthy could own them, and even then, only to use them for hunting.

While England and France wanted to control the availability of weapons to the citizenry, they also sought to create standing militias loyal to the government. At this time, wars were commonly fought with ships rather than armies, and so they continued to put more money into their fleets, but raised small standing armies as well.

When the colonists originally came to North America, many settlers owned guns. However, they used their guns to kill for food to survive, rather than for sport. The guns were also used as protection against Native American attackers, as well as other European settlers. When the need for guns increased in times of hostility, all males were allowed to own them for the sake of protection. As the colonies grew, so did the number of guns and gun owners.

Just as in Europe, the leaders of the colonies realized the danger of allowing so many people to own guns. Many settlers were selling their guns to the Native Americans for astounding profits. When the leaders discovered this, they too, like their European counterparts, enacted strict legislation controlling the availability and transferability of guns. Anyone caught selling one to a Native would be hanged.

However, that did not stop many from establishing gun-trading rings with Native Americans. Dutch and English settlers alike, all through the country, were selling weapons to Natives, arming them. Death penalties were threatened and carried out by leaders of both countries, to no avail.

The English government, however, maintained a gun trade with the Iroquois tribe. A purely political move, the English continued to do so to play a role in wars between various tribes. Playing off the anger of the Iroquois, who despised the Dutch, who only sold weapons to the Mohicans and the Mohawks, the English ignited even more violence among the tribes. Because the Dutch and English publicly opposed the sale of guns to natives, but privately involved themselves in those acts, suspicions of treason and confusion about who to trust rose to an incredible high during that period. Laws were established prohibiting trade with anyone from any nation who sold weapons to Natives; but again, the sales continued.

In an attempt to demonstrate some semblance of authority over the gun trafficking, in 1676, the Virginia Assembly began to allow the sale of guns to Natives, provided the sellers had a permit to do so.

Throughout the 1700's, new laws in the colonies prohibited gun sales to blacks, in an attempt to exude control over slaves, and prevent a rebellion of any kind. Furthermore, freed slaves were never even allowed to join a militia, even when soldiers were in desperate need.

Guns were always in constant demand and need. Crime became prevalent in many colonies, and so the need for self-defense rose as well. In August of 1767, hundreds of armed men decided to attack communities where criminals lived, and over time, succeeded in eradicating a great deal of them. Then they began to attack debtors and those they perceived to be undesirable members of society. About a year later, government officials established officers of the law, and the vigilantes disbanded.

In the 1770's, as the colonies and England verged on war, Parliament placed an embargo on the sale of guns and ammunition to colonists. When the colonists defied the ban, British troops were sent to enforce the law. General Thomas Gage, the British commander in Boston, ordered hundreds of troops to take away the weapons of those who violated the ban, and arrest their leaders. The battles that ensued after, in Lexington and Concord, paved the way for the Revolutionary War.

After these battles, Congress created the Continental Army, and placed George Washington in its command. Congress also asked all the militias to join together and unite for the cause of the Revolution. However, the Army consisted of untrained soldiers, without the knowledge or experience of fighting in a war. During the initial phase of the War, when there were few battles fought, the soldiers would waste what little gunpowder they had. They would shoot geese for food, and often shot each other for fun. Many people also deserted the Army, and took the weapons with them.

Debates ensued over whose responsibility it was to provide the soldiers with arms- the national, state, or local government. Concurrently, laws were taking effect all over the country governing the use of firearms. As colonial charters became invalid, states began to draft their own constitutions, demonstrating their distrust of a national government. These Constitutions gave citizens the rights to own firearms to ensure that the government never assumes too much power over its citizens.

However, when the Revolution ended, there was still a need for a permanent army. Invading forces of Native Americans and debtor uprisings had proven that the need for an army was critical to maintain law and order in the colonies. As various factious armies began to suppress rebellions, the dissatisfaction with the government grew as well. Change was necessary for the survival of the country.

Congress called for a convention to revise the Articles of Confederation, but those who attended quickly realized they would need to construct an entirely new system of government. Debates raged over whether or not to construct a national Army, or delegate such duties to the states individually, and allow them to control their own forces. Fearful of standing national armies, reminiscent of the French and Roman empires, the delegates decided that there ought to be mandatory militias in all states. However, they divided the power to control them between the federal and state governments. They gave the states the right to train them, but allowed the national government to decide when they should be used.

When the Constitution went to the various states for ratification, many still opposed it, because they felt it gave too much power to the centralized, federal government. People feared the government, in turn, would seek to limit the rights and freedoms of the people, and exert more control over the militias. As a result, a Bill of Rights was drafted in compromise, and the Constitution was ratified. The real compromise was the Second Amendment, which would cause extreme controversy for centuries. On the one hand, the federal government would still be able to summon the armies of the states; on the other, the unforeseen battle over personal gun rights lay ahead of them.

Mankind has been in a constant cycle of weapon making. From the beginning of time, crude weapons of stone and wood were used for the survival of the human race. As centuries passed, man's fascination and needs fueled a new global culture- the one we now know as the Gun Culture. Centuries have passed, but the fixation on weapons and destruction remains the same. New breakthroughs in science and technology throughout the millennia have fueled this desire for deadly weapons, and as portable weapons became more readily available in the Middle Ages, people began to stock and use them. Whether for sport, survival, or crime, the world's weapons have ultimately wreaked havoc on its people. In the 1700's, the world thought it had seen the height of the destruction that these weapons would ever cause. The Revolution that loomed on the horizon, and more importantly, the Constitution that followed, and the controversy that would last for centuries, demonstrated that the world had seen but a fraction of the devastation that was to come.

THE EARLY AMERICAN GUN CULTURE

In the 1790's, the government set about to form a national Army; mindful, however, that it was the state's responsibility to oversee such a force. To this end, Congress passed several laws to boost the size of its armies. One such law required every man between the ages of 18 and 45 to enroll in a militia. Only one in five militiamen actually owned their own guns, and about half of the guns the government distributed were broken.

Secretary of War Henry Knox lobbied for Americans to begin making their own guns, and urged Congress to assist. By reducing the dependence on foreign supplies of weapons, he reasoned, America would be more independent and able to fight for itself. Congress passed several measures to begin the construction of arsenals to manufacture weapons and ammunition.

Throughout the 1790's and early 1800's, the government continued to heavily invest in firearms and banned the exportation of arms several times. In time, the government also began paying for the weapons its soldiers used, and eliminated their requirement for the soldiers to use their own. Also, many of the militias began to refer to themselves as the National Guard, a sign that hinted at the need for a national army, to be used to solve national problems.

As time passed, the new nation had many problems with its militias. Most members were poorly trained, and many didn't even know how to use a gun. By the War of 1812, the problem became so great, that the government began considering the institution of a draft. During the War, the situation deteriorated to the point where troops were fleeing the battlefields before the fighting had even begun.

At this time, the practice of dueling in America began to take hold like never before. Men, claiming to be fighting for their honor, would challenge others who had insulted or harmed them. More often than not, the man who was challenged accepted, and a duel was scheduled. The most famous duel in history was between Aaron Burr and Alexander Hamilton, the latter of whom died as a result. Andrew Jackson, a military hero who would eventually become president, was infamous for dueling, and killed several people during those confrontations.

Many times, dueling did not automatically mean death for one man or another. Serious injuries would sometimes result, and many times none of the men were even injured. However, many times, duels did result in death, often when the duel was made in response to a serious incident, which made both men literally want to kill each other, and at the end of the duel, one did. As a result of all the deaths and injuries that occurred because of dueling, many Americans called on their leaders to put an end to the horrific practice.

Many states did enact legislation that banned dueling, though their efficiency has never been proven. Illegal dueling continued on long after the laws had been made, much to the chagrin of anti-dueling groups. Ironically, their continued dueling fueled an even greater effort on the part of those groups. They lobbied officials to pass legislation to crack down even harder on duelers, and also to prevent people from getting guns entirely, not just limiting the usage of guns. Even today, many people incite others by challenging them to duels, though they have no real intention of carrying them out. U.S. Senator Zell Miller, for instance, challenged a cable news personality to a duel in 2004, just for questioning him about his political endorsements.

Manufacturing of weapons in America began to take hold at this time as well. Many began creating weapons with interchangeable parts, making it easier to fix broken guns, rather than having to replace them. The advances in technology enabled gun manufacturers to produce more weapons, which made it easier for people to get them.

As immigrants moved to America, many of the natural-born White Americans did not like the idea of having foreigners join American militias and take up arms. They joined groups that opposed militias and the draft on the basis of their practicality. The result of those efforts was the breakdown of the militia system in America, to the point where militias were few, and even then, only voluntary. Because of this, militias were composed of upper class Americans, who had the time to learn how to use firearms. This kept firearms out of the hands of the foreigners they despised so much.

As the number and size of militias continued to decrease, more efforts were made to build a regular army. This changed signaled a shift in domestic security policy in many ways. Chief among them was the near elimination of the rationalization for private gun ownership. Since private gun ownership had previously been necessary for the buildup of militias, now that militias became nearly extinct, the basis of legal gun ownership had almost been eliminated.

It is possible that private gun ownership may have been declared illegal at that point, were it not for the fact that the rise in personal gun use had little to do with security. As militias began to recede, citizens took up arms for sporting activities instead. Hunting had become the new fad in America for the middle class. Magazines dedicated to hunting began publication, and because of the high prices of weapons, gun ownership became a sign of elitism and superiority.

On January 30, 1835, President Andrew Jackson left the chamber of the U.S House of Representatives. As he was leaving, Richard Lawrence, an ordinary citizen, fired two pistols at the president, but both miraculously misfired. In this incident, the consequences of gun abuse were benign to its intended victim. Across the country, however, gun owners took to concealing their weapons with fatal consequences. Spontaneous shootings were taking place across America, and a tidal wave of concern swept the nation.

Reformers lobbied their state legislatures to enact legislation that would control gun use. Many states did pass laws, and they became the first meaningful gun control acts in the nation's history. They limited the use of concealed weapons, and the punishments became more severe against those who decided to continue to use them.

The first debate on gun control ensued, with gun owners claiming their Second Amendment rights were being violated. Challenges against the early legislation were taken to courts, but were upheld on the basis that the Second Amendment only protected people from federal control over guns. State laws were excluded from the protection of the Second Amendment.

In the early 1800's, protection against those who abused the primitive gun control laws fell on local officials, such as sheriffs and constables. Before there were ever organized police forces, illegal sale and ownership of handguns increased. They were used for a variety of reasons; to spur and elongate riots in big cities, to settle personal disputes, even for racial reasons. Whites would buy guns to use against free and enslaved blacks, and blacks would buy guns to defend themselves against them. Much of the possession of guns was done in the name of "self-defense", though the facts of the time clearly prove that their true motives were far different.

The further advancement of gun-making technologies, as well as its widespread applications, made it easier for private citizens to buy these weapons. When the U.S. went to war with Mexico in 1846, the government gave contracts to private gun makers like Colt and Remington to supply the military with handguns for the war. The large contracts spurred enormous growth in the gun industry, and indirectly caused private gun ownership to take hold in greater numbers than ever. Gun companies found that civilians were offering more money for their guns than the government was, and became an even greater source for profit than their large government orders were. Corporate expansion of the gun industry was inevitable at this time, and new companies began to take hold and flourish.

Another effect of this latest expansion of the gun trade was economical. Guns were previously prized possessions, not just because of the potency they possessed in their ability to inflict harm, but because of their high price and value as well. As the gun companies began to make more money from their government and citizen clients, the need to charge exorbitant rates for their products decreased. As a result, when companies began charging less for firearms, they made it easier for poor people to purchase them. This was perhaps the single greatest factor in the expansion of private gun ownership in this time period.

This apparent gun frenzy in America had many effects. Firstly, the rise in gun ownership changed American society. It had now become a major part of American life, reaching across all demographics and areas of the country. Because of the many applications firearms had, it became evident at the time that everyone had a reason to own one. Ownership of a gun became a sign of manhood and machismo, and even young men in their teens began to tout them wherever they went.

Additionally, the increase in the manufacture of guns by American companies made it possible for the United States to stop relying on foreign nations for their supply of firearms. Instead, in the 1850's, American gun companies began to supply the world with firearms of their own.

As sectional differences began to rise in America, those in the North and South began to stockpile an arsenal of firearms. When the Civil War broke out, both sides began fighting with the guns they had, and relied on volunteers to fight. Soon though, the need for more soldiers was apparent to both sides, and a draft was instituted. As a result of the increase in the number of soldiers fighting, there were very few arms to meet the demands of the growing armies. Once again, the government began importing firearms, and the South joined them soon after.

During this time, there were many incidents of violent citizen reaction against the draft. In cities and towns across the country, government officials attempting to enforce the law sought those who refused to show up for the draft. Violent riots broke out in New York, Boston, Detroit, Philadelphia, and many other locales. Citizens armed themselves in these riots, and the consequences were deadly.

These actions did not stop with the ending of the Civil War. On April 14, 1865, John Wilkes Booth used his pistol to assassinate President Abraham Lincoln with a single shot to the back of his head. This violent act followed the deadliest war that ever took place on American soil. The Civil War was fought without the modern technologies we have today; without air power, missiles, or the myriad of other high-tech weapons we now have in our military arsenal. It became clear that there was truly only one cause for the massive death and devastation that took place over the four years of the war- the mass availability and possession of the one weapon they did have- the gun.

MODERN AMERICAN GUN CULTURE

In the period following the Civil War, racial tensions in America reached a breaking point. The passage of the 13th and 14th Amendments, besides giving African Americans civil rights, gave them the right to own guns. As they proceeded to buy guns, southern whites did everything in their power to stop them, including murdering those blacks that tried to exercise their new rights. Riots erupted across the South as former Confederate soldiers joined others as they fought against blacks, killing those who owned guns as well as those who didn't.

Societies began to form aimed at killing African Americans who tried to exercise any of their civil rights. These included the Ku Klux Klan, the Knights of White Camellia, and other white supremacist organizations. Their actions forced Congress to pass the Ku Klux Klan Act, which made it a federal crime to commit designated acts of crime. Since the local officials were as corrupt as the people who committed such crimes, the federal government stepped in to ensure the protection of the civil rights of all people.

However, this did not stop violence against African Americans. Vigilantes still took to the streets en masse, killing blacks for a myriad of supposed reasons that were concocted to justify their violence. These ranged from general defense to accusing blacks of different crimes, some of which were never even committed. These racial witch-hunts always resulted in slayings of African Americans, but the new laws provided that the federal government would be able to take control of these situations, which they did. Unfortunately, many lives were lost in the interim.

As Americans moved westward, they required more guns. Natives in the West were plentiful, and the settlers argued they needed to defend themselves against them. In big cities in the West, new organizations of vigilantes were formed to combat supposed threats of crime. Some cities passed laws against carrying guns entirely. At the same time, other cities and states freely gave their residents guns to fight the Natives.

These actions led to major events in the gun control movement in America. As Americans who went westward armed themselves to a greater degree than ever before, large pockets of violence began to take hold in large cities and towns in that region. While the government declared such places to be in a "state of insurrection", it seemed they had little success in controlling the gun-toting settlers and cowboys. However, ranchers decided to take action. They stopped hiring anyone who openly carried guns, and this led to a major decrease in the number of armed people, and the number of guns in general, in the West.

The meteoric increase in gun ownership in the mid-19th Century forced states to take decisive action in controlling it, and enforcing the gun control laws already in place. To do this, in 1877, states formed the National Guard Association, a new type of militia used to enforce the laws. The National Guard grew quickly, and many citizens feared that this would lead to a more oppressive government- one controlled by standing armies, as had been the case in Europe. In response, citizens organized their own groups to advance the causes of gun ownership, and resist what they believed to be laws enforced by a military-led government.

When the Spanish-American War began in 1898, the National Guard was called to serve. Though they had no real experience fighting in major wars, they did so, and the war lasted for a short period of time before an American victory was declared.

Only a few years later, President Theodore Roosevelt pushed Congress to change the way the National Guard worked. He wanted to have a ready, well-trained standing Army to fight should it be necessary to do so. In 1903, Congress changed the National Guard to be an official militia, and required all men between 18 and 45 to serve in a "reserve" militia. The funding for the Guard was also split between the federal and state governments, and allowed the president to call on the Guard at any time. Five years later, Congress acted again to transform the National Guard, by allowing the government to deploy members of the Guard to foreign countries to fight, and to decide how long they would stay there.

After the reform of the National Guard, states across the country moved to improve their gun control laws. Some states decided on stiff penalties for the concealment of guns; in states where that wasn't a major issue, laws were passed requiring gun owners to secure special permits for the ownership of guns. Failure to do so resulted in steep fines, and even some jail time. As the issue aroused more action and state regulation of guns in the early years of the 20th Century, Congress began to act on the international front.

As war waged on in Mexico, gun dealers began selling weapons to all fighters there who would pay for them. In response, in 1912, Congress passed a law giving the president the power to control international arms trades at his discretion. President William H. Taft immediately banned all arms sales to Mexico, and the new law brought fines and jail time to those who violated it. At that time, it was the strongest gun control law ever created; more stringent than any law created for the domestic sale or use of guns inside the United States.

In 1919, the Eighteenth Amendment to the Constitution, banning the sale of alcohol in the United States, was ratified. The ratification of this amendment led to the regulation of an industry that essentially was impossible to regulate. Government bureaucracies were made to enforce this law, but as bootlegging activities increased, and the methods of bootleggers became more secretive and complex, it became apparent that the government's attempt at Prohibition was a failure.

The bootlegging itself gave way to an enormous increase in the crime rate across the country, most notably in Chicago. The reason for this was the newfound control of organized crime that was taking hold in big cities. As the twenties progressed, these gangsters became more prolific, and their control of bootlegging activities earned them more money and allowed them to pursue other avenues of crime. As the crime statistics reflected, gun crimes continued to soar, and more citizens and government officials saw the need to do something to control the seemingly hopeless situation.

As government officials continued to crack down on bootleggers, more and more criminals stepped forward to take their place. Enforcement became difficult, if not impossible, because as more and more small time violators were caught, the courts did not have the time to prosecute all the offenders. Meanwhile, the mobsters were the ones who controlled this newfound lucrative, illegal trade, and their hold strengthened each day.

Naturally, gun crimes rose during this time as well. Many bills were proposed before Congress to curb the gun trade in America, but all failed to pass, some never making it out of hearings of the Congressional committees to which it was designated, which is the first step in passing any piece of legislation. The reason for this was simple- though many constituents supported gun control, many more opposed it, and more importantly, their representatives in Congress did too.

Many began attacking the various gun magazines, blaming them for the increase in gun ownership, and therefore, albeit indirectly, the rise in gun crime. Mail order catalogs, which offered people cheap guns at cheap prices, sold thousands of guns a year, and were also to blame. Finally, in February of 1927, Congress passed a bill that banned magazines or any literature that was sent through the public mail system that included advertisements for guns.

The governor of New York at the time, himself a gun control advocate, was Franklin Delano Roosevelt. Roosevelt began a campaign for the presidency, and as part of his platform, he promised to make gun crime a federal issue, and to deal with it on a national level. On the basis of this promise and many others, he went on to win the presidential election of 1932.

On February 14, 1933, before he went in front of a large crowd to speak, Giuseppe Zangara, a mentally disturbed anarchist, fired a gun at Roosevelt. He missed the president-elect, but injured five others, including the mayor of Chicago, who died a few days later from those injuries. When Roosevelt assumed the presidency less than a month later, his earlier support of gun control coupled with his assassination attempt motivated him even further to address the growing problem.

Roosevelt reshaped a government organization into the Federal Bureau of Investigation. One of its first priorities was to study and propose ways to deal with the growing gun culture in America. The results of those efforts came in the form of several gun control proposals. As more massacres took place, like the St. Valentines Day Massacre, and other mob-related incidents, more people supported the measures, and with the backing of the president, they were proposed before Congress.

Congress acted, and in 1934, passed laws giving the federal government power to prosecute those who murdered federal agents or extorted money through interstate means. Not wanting to interfere too much with local regulation and enforcement, the FBI began prosecuting such cases slowly and deliberately. That year, they also apprehended and killed several mobsters, including "Baby Face"

Nelson, and more notably, the infamous bank robber John Dillinger.

As these actions were taken, popular opinion flowed to the government in support of regulating guns, and enforcing and even creating new gun control laws. More proposed legislation made its way to Congress, but the NRA, which was stronger than ever, met these new proposals with fierce resistance. Many bills failed to pass, but one major piece of reform did.

On June 26, 1934, Congress passed the National Firearms Act, which was the strongest gun control measure ever enacted. It made the weapons used by gangsters, most notably, the sawed-off shotgun and submachine gun, illegal. It required all gun dealers to pay a firearm tax, and register with the government. The registration process itself was thorough- it required fingerprinting, extensive background checks, and heavy taxes to register.

Four years later, Congress passed the Federal Firearms Act of 1938. This mandated that those who traded guns internationally or between states had to get a federal license. It also banned convicts from getting guns through interstate means, and punished those who did not have all the necessary permits and licenses to sell guns.

The most famous Supreme Court case dealing with these laws came in 1939, in *United States v. Miller*. In this case, Jack Miller carried an unregistered shotgun from Oklahoma to Arkansas in violation of the Federal Firearms Act. The defendant argued that the law violated his Second Amendment rights, but the Supreme Court disagreed, saying that Miller's possession of the weapon did not "contribute to the common defense". His actions were therefore illegal, and not protected under the Second Amendment since he was not part of a militia.

When World War II broke out, President Roosevelt did not ask Congress to authorize a draft. Instead, he used the National Guard to fight the War. During the War, civilian gun use increased for training purposes, and gun manufacturers filled the biggest orders for guns the industry had ever seen. This massive influx of guns into society, as well as the new idealization of the gun, contributed to an increase in civilian crime, and stalled the gun control movement in America for some time.

After the War, there was a notably diminished interest on the part of the citizenry and the government to pursue any further gun control measures. The War brought about social changes in the way people perceived and thought about guns. They once again became a symbol of machismo and manhood, and despite the ever-increasing rate at which gun crimes were being committed, public interest in going after the issue waned.

More parents began to believe the propaganda issued by the gun advocacy groups, which suggested that teaching children to use guns at an early age was good for their character, and would enable them to serve their country in the military. Magazines promoting gun use took off, and readership levels rose to new heights.

Membership in gun groups was no longer limited to the few who could afford guns; with the influx of cheap guns into the United States after the War, everyone could afford to buy one, and joined groups of people who shared their zeal for this hobby. New movies were produced featuring gun-slinging heroes, and new television shows were created with gun violence as the central theme.

As a result of the growing power of the gun lobby, through the 1950's and early 1960's, dozens of gun control measures were defeated, and like before, many of these bills did not make it past the preliminary hearings of Congressional Committees.

It was only until the assassination of President John F. Kennedy that people began to realize the growing epidemic of dangerous gun use, and the need to control it. Instantly, the public's opinion of gun control shifted from one of fierce opposition to strong support, favoring any measures that would stem gun violence.

The Civil Rights movement also witnessed tragedies because of easily available guns. In 1965, civil rights leaders and protestors were being shot in the streets in areas all over the country. The Watts riots in Los Angeles pinned white police against black protestors, and resulted in fierce looting, and the deaths of more than 30 people, and injuries sustained by 1,000 more.

Racial tensions caused major violence across the country in the mid-1960's, as radicals on both sides took to the streets brandishing weapons, and in one instance, stormed the chamber of the California State Assembly. Despite these incidents, and the outcry of the public as well as President Lyndon Baines Johnson, the gun lobby continued to stall legislation time and again.

In 1968, the assassinations of Martin Luther King, Jr. and presidential candidate Robert F. Kennedy turned the country once and for all over the tide of opposition, and they called unequivocally for some semblance of meaning-ful reform. Ideas about strengthening loopholes, stricter requirements to obtain gun licenses and a crackdown on the interstate gun trade, led to major debates in Congress. The time was right for a comprehensive act of Congress that would rein in the violence of the time. The time had come, many believed, and the result of the debates was the passage of the Gun Control Act of 1968. (For a deeper analysis of the measure, see "Gun Control Laws", a later chapter in this book.)

After the passage of this bill, the nation's attention turned towards Vietnam. Johnson focused too much on the war, and when Richard Nixon became president, he opposed regulating international gun commerce, hoping to arm foreigners with guns and use them to win the Vietnam War. His plan proved unsuccessful, and the continued failure of the government to press for more gun regula-tions in the wake of the 1968 Act led to another increase in crime.

In the early 1970's, murder rates rose even as crime rates as a whole fell. Almost 10,000 murders a year were com-mitted with handguns, and another 2,000 were commit-ted with other guns. Yet, the fierce opposition of the gun advocacy groups to tighter regulation of handguns in particular, remained strong. Fortunately, the American people differed, and polls reflected the desire of a major-ity of Americans to have mandated gun registration. Additionally, more than a third of the public wanted to ban handguns outright.

In late 1975, two attempted assassinations made against President Gerald Ford, both committed by unstable women, placed the issue of tighter gun regulation to the forefront of the national agenda. The issue played a large role in the 1976 presidential campaign, and as a result of the nation's growing crime rate, social activism on both sides of the issue rose dramatically. The NRA's membership continued to grow, and more organizations were formed to combat the growing gun culture and support tougher gun control laws. Yet again, as in the past, no pieces of landmark legislation made its way to the Congress.

After the attempted assassination of President Ronald Reagan on March 30, 1981 (discussed in more detail in the chapter "Gun Control Laws"), people from both sides of the issue used the shooting to bolster their arguments. Those who supported gun control said that the attempted assassination proved once again the need for stronger gun control measures. Those who opposed gun control used Reagan's later comments criticizing gun control, saying that despite his assassination attempt, the president continued to support unrestricted gun ownership.

Despite the fact that no significant legislation was prepared on a national level, there was movement on a local level in at least one village in the country. In Morton Grove, Illinois, an attempt to open up a gun shop near a school was met with fierce resistance by the public. In response, the local government acted to ban most guns in the village. The ban was later challenged in a federal court, but was upheld. Unfortunately, similar laws were not passed in other locales.

In 1982, the public had a chance to weigh in on the issue when referendums were proposed in several states. In California, there was a proposition that would require the registration of handguns, and create a ban on concealable and mail order weapons. The measures failed to pass by wide margins on Election Day, giving greater credibility to the pro-gun lobby.

Throughout the 1980's, another significant tool in the gun control battle became more prevalent. The pro- and anti-gun lobbies campaigned heavily across the country for candidates who supported their views on the issue. The most successful way of getting their candidates elected was by making large campaign donations in races for all levels of government. Through this means, the strength of the gun lobby was seen clearly, as evidenced by the amount of money they raised for candidates. They consistently out raised and outspent those on the other side of the issue, and therefore had many more victorious candidates than did the pro-gun control organizations.

In the 1988 presidential campaign, the gun lobby supported George Bush for the presidency because the Democratic candidate, Michael Dukakis, had a fiercely anti-gun record as Governor of Massachusetts. Though the gun lobby was not as enthusiastic for Bush as they were for Reagan, they supported him because they knew Dukakis would crack down on weapons abuse if elected. Their efforts on behalf of Bush contributed to his victory on Election Day.

In the wake of a string of gun shootings in the late 1980's, Congress acted to limit the importation of semiautomatic weapons. More efforts were made to ban assault weapons as well, particularly the AK-47, which was used in recent shootings, most notably in a shooting at a California school. As some measures passed, the NRA spent millions to oppose others, calling such proposals "massive government intrusion in people's lives". Many later bills aimed at banning the most dangerous weapons failed because of the efforts of the gun lobby.

The failure to ban assault weapons at that time contributed to the massive devastation that was to follow. On April 29, 1992, four white California police officers were acquitted on charges stemming from beating Rodney King. The acquittal was immediately followed by massive riots throughout Los Angeles. Thousands of guns were purchased, used, and stashed away as the riots continued. Both blacks and whites were responsible for shootings, and dozens of people were killed. Damage was in the hundreds of millions of dollars, and once again the failure to ban these weapons led to yet another disaster that could have been averted.

In August of 1992, Randy Weaver was charged with illegally selling two sawed off shotguns. He failed to appear in court for those charges, and threatened to kill anyone who would try to apprehend him. BATF (Bureau of Alcohol, Tobacco, and Firearms) agents surrounded his cabin in Ruby Ridge, Idaho, and during the course of a shootout, killed his wife and son. When he finally was apprehended, agents found an arsenal of weapons in his cabin.

In February of 1993, BATF agents once again surrounded a compound they believed was being used for illegal gun trafficking in Waco, Texas. The Branch Davidian compound there housed men, women, and children, and was led by David Koresh, their self-proclaimed leader. When agents came to arrest him, the people inside the compound fired at them, killing four agents. A standoff lasted for weeks thereafter, until agents stormed the compound on April 19, 1993. Fire broke out, and in the melee, over 75 people lost their lives. Like after Ruby Ridge, the agents found a large cache of weapons in the compound, including assault weapons.

After Bill Clinton became president in early 1993, he proposed several tough gun control measures to the Congress. He signed numerous executive orders that made it harder for people to buy guns. He also endorsed a popular new proposal, the Brady Bill. The Brady Bill cracked down on specific weapons, and was considered a great victory for the supporters of gun control (discussed in more detail in the chapter "Gun Control Laws"). Another victory soon followed.

On September 13, 1994, the president signed the Violent Crime Control and Law Enforcement Act. The law was originally met with fierce opposition by Republicans who were threatened by the Republican National Committee to vote against the bill or risk losing the support of the party. Despite this, many Republicans did vote for it, and the bill, which included a ban on many assault weapons, passed the Congress.

Throughout the mid-1980's and the mid-1990's, gun related deaths among young people more than doubled. The new laws were just beginning to take effect, but public sentiment began to shift favorably for gun control. Membership in the NRA shifted as a result of its zero-tolerance policy for any and all gun control legislation. Members of Congress that supported the NRA lost in the 1996 elections, and Bill Clinton was reelected as well.

The 1990's also saw the rise of media violence; carnage was displayed openly in video games and movies. The influence of the growing violent culture yielded terrible results. School shootings by students occurred often, and all across the nation. In July 1998, a distraught man fired a gun in the U.S. Capitol building, and killed two guards. Scenes of mayhem around the nation in schools, workplaces, and neighborhoods, all contributed to the growing complacency Americans felt towards violence.

At the height of this tide of violence came the worst school shooting in the nation's history. On April 20, 1999, the Columbine High School massacre took the lives of 15 people. As the nation mourned like never before, a new proposal was put forth that would require a three-day waiting period so that a background check could be done on anybody wanting to buy a gun at a gun show. The bill passed the Senate a month after the Columbine shooting.

In the 2000 Election, the Democrats nominated Vice President Al Gore, who cast the tie-breaking vote in the Senate to mandate background checks for gun show purchases. The Republicans chose Texas Governor George W. Bush, who signed a law allowing people to carry concealed weapons. Bush had close ties with the NRA, and their supporters became his supporters. The issue did not carry much weight in that election, and in the months following Bush's inauguration, little was done to revive past gun control measures.

In the wake of the September 11th, 2001 attacks, terrorism took priority over all other issues. Domestic policy was pushed aside for the most part, and an effort to prevent future terrorist attacks was the primary concern of all Americans.

Yet, even today, shootings occur at schools in America; they happen in our businesses, in our communities, and they have becomes so commonplace that they have been accepted as an unfortunate fact of life. The gun culture has existed in America since this nation's birth. Society and culture have shaped our views of violence and gun use as acceptable. When the cost of such use is human life, it certainly is not acceptable. It does not have to be that way.

Many will argue that this issue does not deserve the attention of our government. They argue that many bills were passed; yet the violence continues. On the one hand, those critics may be right. In the end, we will never know unless we once again make a constructive effort to stem the tide of gun violence in America- for our neighborhoods, for ourselves, and for our children.

PART II:

THE SAD TRUTH

THE CASES

In February of 1992, in Thomas Jefferson High School, in Brooklyn, New York, a ninth-grader entered the school with a gun. While the students were changing classes, he fatally shot two students in the hallway of the school.

That same month, at Roland Park Elementary School, in Baltimore, Maryland, a police officer confiscated a pager from a seventh grader. In retaliation for this, the student shot the officer.

In March of 1992, an eight-year-old boy brought a gun to his school in Chicago, Illinois. He had put it in his book bag, thinking it was only a toy. He then shot and paralyzed an eight-year-old girl in his classroom.

In May of 1992, in Lindhurst High School, in Olivehurst, California, Eric Houston, a twenty-two year old student, was angry with a teacher who gave him a failing grade that kept him from graduating. He walked onto the campus armed with a shotgun and a rifle. He killed the teacher, Robert Brens, three students, and injured eleven other students. He then held 59 students and teachers hostage during an eight-hour siege.

In September of 1992, in Palo Duro High School, in Amarillo, Texas, a teenager got into a fight. He then shot six students in school, and two of them were critically injured.

In December 1992, Wayne Lo, an eighteen-year-old honor student at Simon's Rock College, carried a modified AK-47 assault rifle through the snowy Berkshire mountains campus in Great Barrington, Massachusetts. He opened fire, killing Professor Nacanan Saez, and eighteen-year-old Galen Gibson, a student from Gloucester, Massachusetts. Four other students were injured, but they all survived.

In February 1993, a dozen teenagers watched as fifteen-year-old Robert Heard killed seventeen-year-old classmate Michael Shean Ensley at Reseda High School in California. Heard, a Reseda High football player, confronted Ensley in a corridor during a midmorning snack break. He fired once, hitting Ensley in the chest. Ensley staggered outside and collapsed in a grassy area near the administration office. At first, several witnesses thought it was only a harmless act, but upon realizing that Ensley had actually been shot, they rushed him to the nurse's office. He was pronounced dead a short time later at Northridge Medical Center.

Heard fled the campus, but was apprehended by a school police officer. He was carrying a small-caliber handgun. Ensley's mother later said that he had enrolled at Reseda to escape the Los Angeles urban gangs. After the incident, many students expressed an unwillingness to return to their classes.

In March 1993, an eleven-year-old boy threatened a classmate with an unloaded BB pistol at Herrick Avenue Elementary School in Sylmar, California. He was later expelled, because police said that he had pointed the gun at his classmate, and threatened to kill her and her family.

Shortly after that, thirteen teenagers were expelled for bringing guns to school. Sixteen other students had been previously dropped from the system, including a twelve-year-old middle school student who was caught carrying a BB gun in school. In Omaha, Nebraska, a fourteen-year-old boy held a gun to the head of a fifth grader. School officials disciplined him, and a few months later, he shot and killed a thirteen-year-old girl with a .45 caliber automatic. There was no known motive for the killing, but many suspected that he was upset about the prior incident he had in school, and he wanted to get revenge.

In a small Kentucky town, a seventeen-year-old boy walked into class, and fatally shot his English teacher with a revolver. Upon hearing the shot, a custodian rushed into the classroom, and found the boy aiming his gun at a girl. He pushed her down and was killed by the bullet that was meant for her. Teachers who had gathered outside the classroom pulled the dead custodian in the hallway. The shooter held his classmates hostage for more than fifteen minutes. Finally, he released the students, and surrendered to police.

On October 1, 1997, in Pearl, Mississippi, sixteen-year-old Luke Woodham killed his own mother. He then went to his school, and randomly shot whomever he saw. He killed three people, and wounded seven.

On December 1, 1997, a high school prayer meeting was taking place in West Paducah, Kentucky. Fourteen-year-old Michael Carneal entered, carrying a gun. He opened fire, and killed three students.

On March 24, 1998, two boys, Mitchell Johnson, age 13, and Andrew Golden, age 11, set off the fire alarm at their school in Jonesboro, Arkansas, and shot at their schoolmates as they filed out of the building. Together, the boys had three rifles and seven pistols. They fired twenty-two shots in less than four minutes, killing four students. They also killed teacher Shannon Wright, who gave her life shielding one of her students. No doubt this student will be forever grateful for her sacrifice. Golden and Johnson also wounded ten other people, mostly children.

On April 24, 1998, exactly one month after the shooting in Arkansas, there was a school dance in Edinboro, Pennsylvania. As everyone danced inside the school, fourteen-year-old Andrew Wurst entered the dance floor. He was armed, and opened fire. When he stopped shooting, he had killed a teacher.

On May 21, 1998, a fifteen-year-old boy named Kip Kinkel was preparing for a massacre in Springfield, Oregon. While at home, he killed both his parents. He then proceeded to go to school during the scheduled lunch break. He entered the school through the cafeteria entrance, and sprayed a hail of bullets at the students there. He had shot twenty-four classmates in total; twenty-two were injured, and two were killed.

Perhaps the most infamous school shooting took place on April 20, 1999. Eric Harris, 18, and Dylan Klebold, 17, arrived at Columbine High School in Littleton, Colorado, wearing their usual black trench coats. However, it wasn't the trench coats they wore that were unusual; it was what those coats were covering. They carried an arsenal of weapons, including two sawed-off 12-gauge shotguns, a 9-mm semiautomatic rifle, and a TEC-DC 9-mm semiautomatic handgun.

They entered the school, and with no warning, fired at athletes, minorities, and others. Students hid under desks and tables, and behind locked doors, to avoid getting shot at. Many people hid in the library, and many were killed there. Police estimated that Harris and Klebold fired 900 rounds of ammunition in their one-hour killing spree. In total, twelve students and one teacher were shot dead, as well as Harris and Klebold, who turned their guns on themselves.

On October 19, 2000, in New York City, two 16-year-old high school male students were arrested in the stabbing death of a 12-year-old intermediate school student who had been in the high school cafeteria with a 15-year-old male high school student. The 15-year-old male, who was later arrested when a police officer saw him carrying a .44 Magnum, and the victim, had been fighting in the cafeteria with the two 16-year-olds. The 12-year-old was later stabbed in the chest about a block away from the school. The incident was suspected to be gang-related.

On November 29, 2000, in a San Jose, California High School, a 16-year-old student was stabbed to death in front of his brother, his high school principal, and a number of classmates at a light rail station about a block away from his high school, minutes after school dismissal. The suspects were believed to be four students at the high school.

On December 7, 2000, in San Pablo, California, a sixteen-year-old student was killed after being shot in the neck by someone in a passing car across the street from his high school. He stumbled into the campus in front of administrative offices and was rushed to the hospital, but was pronounced dead on arrival.

On March 22, 2001, in El Cajon, California, an 18-year-old high school senior armed with a 12-guage shotgun and a .22-caliber semiautomatic handgun was arrested for firing shots that hit at least three students and two teachers. A school officer returned fire, shooting the suspect.

On October 18, 2001, in a Bradenton, Florida High School, a sixteen-year-old high school student was allegedly beaten to death by a fellow seventeen-year-old male student in an after-school fight behind a food store near the school. The fight reportedly was arranged during a fifth period class and stemmed from harassment over the victim's recent behavior. The victim died from injuries sustained after his head was beaten against the concrete ground.

On January 15, 2002, in Martin Luther King, Jr. High School, in Manhattan, New York, Vincent Rodriguez, 18, shot two students in the hallway of his school, apparently over an incident where the students teased his girlfriend.

On September 10, 2003, there were three major incidents of school violence reported. In Vicksburg, Mississippi, a 20-year-old male high school junior was charged with murder for allegedly shooting a 20-year-old non-student once in the chest while on an access road near the school's football field. This took place at around 2:30 p.m. while school was still in session. In Chicago, Illinois, a 16-year-old male was charged with killing a 16-year-old male Proviso East High School student. The victim was shot in the chest after leaving the school, which had been dismissed early for a staff development day. Finally, in Fort Worth, Texas, a 16-year-old boy allegedly fatally shot a classmate, and then dumped his body in a nearby construction site.

On November 4, 2003, in Bexar County, Texas, a 17-year-old male high school student was charged with murder for allegedly fatally shooting another 17-year-old male high school student during a street brawl that stemmed from a dispute that had started at Judson High School. Police said that around 3:45 p.m., a group of 8 to 12 males rode their bikes after school to the home of the suspect and then ganged up on him near his home. As the group fought, a resident came out of his home and fired two rounds in the air from a rifle in order to frighten the fighters. The resident put down the gun and the group went to beat up the resident, during which time the suspect reportedly picked up the rifle and fired a shot, hitting the victim in the stomach.

On March 29, 2004 at PSJA High School in Pharr, Texas, a 15-year-old female student was stabbed to death. Doctors reportedly told the family she had been stabbed 12 times. Police took a 16-year-old male into custody. It was believed that a school custodian witnessed the attack. The incident occurred after the students were returning from a University Interscholastic League competition that both of them had been participating in when they arrived at the school by bus and unloaded in the parking lot to wait for parents and family to pick them up.

On December 13, 2004, in Union City, New Jersey, an 18-year-old male high school student was fatally stabbed about four blocks from Emerson High School. His alleged killers were two adult males who used a martial arts type sword with a 15-inch blade to stab him. The victim, an alternative education program student from the high school, was stabbed in the chest and pronounced dead at the hospital. A 15-year-old male high school student was also injured, and suffered a broken nose and a cut across his face.

On March 21, 2005, in Red Lake, Minnesota, 16-year-old male high school student Jeff Weise shot and killed five students, a teacher, a security guard, and himself at his high school. Seven others were reportedly wounded. The student is believed to have also killed his grandfather and grandfather's female companion. That was the deadliest attack since the Columbine High School shootings less than six years before.

On October 27, 2005, in San Leandro, California, a 14-year-old female high school student was shot three times in the back and killed while walking to school just blocks away from her high school. A male, believed to be a non-student between 16 and 18 years old, got out of a car, shot the 14-year-old in the back, and then killed himself in an apparent murder-suicide.

On November 8, 2005, in Jacksboro, Tennessee, a 15-year-old male high school freshman shot and killed an assistant principal in the school. The principal and another assistant were also shot and hospitalized during the incident.

On December 6, 2005, in Garden Grove, California, a 16-year-old male high school student was beaten and then fatally shot in the chest. The victim reportedly was involved in a fight near the school's athletic fields. Reports indicate gang members jumped in to assist the victim, who was being beaten, when a member of the original group pulled a gun and shot the victim. Police arrested six alleged gang members in connection with the murder.

On January 13, 2006, in Longwood, Florida, a 15-year-old male middle school student was shot by the SWAT team after pulling out a gun during class, briefly taking another student hostage, and running through the school. The student isolated himself in a bathroom where he was shot by the SWAT team after he reportedly raised the gun at a deputy. The gun was later found to be a pellet gun that looked similar to a 9-mm handgun; the weapon police believed he had. The student later died from his gunshot wound.

On February 25, 2006, in Milwaukee, Wisconsin, a 13-year-old male elementary school student accidentally fired a gun while showing it to a 12-year-old female student, shooting the girl in the toe. The male was taken into custody and the female was treated for a minor injury.

These cases made national and international news. However, there have been many more cases of youth violence. Many of us have never heard of the other cases in Houston, Chicago, New York, Los Angeles, and Detroit. These remained mostly anonymous. What about the fifteen-year-old Hispanic teen who opened fire with an assault rifle on a street full of kids? What about the fourteen-year-old African American who shot an eighteen-year-old convenience store clerk? Or the sixteen-year-old African American who killed three teens outside his apartment building? How about the fifteen-year-old Asian boy who executed a sixteen-year-old with a single bullet to the head?

Maybe you have not heard of the cases just mentioned. But these incidents happen all the time. They happen every day. For the safety of our children and all the children in this nation, we must act now to prevent these heinous acts from ever happening again. Whether or not you hear about all the incidents, they do happen. If we do not take action to prevent these acts from happening again in the future, they will surely repeat themselves. We do not know who will suffer, but we may even mourn the loss of one of our own.

THE STATISTICS

During the last several years, the number of fifteen-to twenty-four-year-old Americans killed by guns has increased considerably, accounting for more deaths for people that age than all natural causes combined. Here are the statistics:

There are more than 200 million guns that are circulating the United States today. Tragically, too many of those are misused by teenagers and the gun owners themselves. Many teenagers are killed or injured with these deadly weapons. In the 1970 Census, there were an estimated 104 million guns in circulation. There was a population of 203.7 million people, so there was an average of one gun for every two citizens. In the 2000 Census, the population grew to a little more than 281 million, so there was about 1 gun for every 1.4 citizens. At the current rate, in 2030, there will be 384 million guns, and about 387 million people, in the United States of America. That means that there will be a gun for every citizen. There are more and more guns manufactured every year, and soon, there will be more guns than people in this country.

One million Americans have died in firearm homicides, suicides, and unintentional shootings since 1962.

America is losing too many children to gun violence. Between 1979 and 2001, gunfire killed 90,000 children and teens in America.

During the 1980's, guns killed 330,000 people in America. During that decade, more people died from guns than from AIDS.

From 1985 to 1993, murders committed by people over age 25 dropped 20 percent; but they increased 65 percent among 18- to 24-year-olds and increased 165 percent among 14- to 17-year-olds.

Between 1986 and 1992, the total number of children killed by firearms rose by 144 percent.

One week in May 1989, Time magazine decided to look at faces instead of statistics. They kept a tally of all the Americans who died from gunshot wounds that week. Their article listed 464 deaths that week, and the story ran over 30 pages. The profiles of the victims were as follows: men and women; they were white, African American, Asian, and Hispanic. Their ages ranged from two to 87. They were from 42 different states, and they were young and old, and many were poor, sick, and abandoned. They died from accidents, homicides, and suicides.

From 1990 to 1998, firearms were responsible for 21% of deaths of Caucasian teens ages 13-19 in the United States, 64% of deaths for African-American teens, 46% of Hispanic teens, 24% of Native American/Alaska Native teens, and 35% of Asian/Pacific Islander teens.

For the first eight months of the 1991-1992 school year, weapons confiscated from students in the New York City Public School system numbered nearly 2,737. These included guns, knives, box cutters, razors, and other potentially deadly instruments. These weapons were found as a result of the new metal detection program that had been instituted. This program was used in 300 intermediate schools, and about 1,300 high schools.

Another program implemented in the 1990-1991 school year was the confiscation of weapons by the security staff. In all, there were 2,983 weapons and unauthorized items confiscated.

During the 1991-1992 school year, 1,043 weapons, including 405 guns, were confiscated at schools in the 640,000-student Los Angeles School District. The number of discovered guns in schools was up about 17% from the year before. Of the guns that were found, 33 were taken from elementary school children, 158 from junior high students, and 182 from senior high school students. There are even more weapons taken to school every day, but they are not found by the authorities.

In 1992, handguns killed 33 people in Great Britain, 36 in Sweden, 97 in Switzerland, 60 in Japan, 13 in Australia, 128 in Canada, and 13,200 in the United States.

The National School Boards Association estimates that in 1993, more than 135,000 guns were brought into U.S. schools each day.

Each year from 1993 to 1997, 1,621 killers under the age of 18 committed gun murders.

Annual rates of firearm homicides for young people between the ages of 15 and 19 increased 155% between 1989 and 1994.

According to the National Education Association, between 1994 and 1999, there were 220 school associated violent events resulting in 253 deaths. 74.5% of these involved firearms. Handguns caused almost 60% of these deaths.

Direct and indirect costs of gun violence in 1995 amounted to more than $14 billion, over 80 percent of which was picked up by taxpayers.

The estimated cost of direct health care expenditures for firearm-related injuries in the US in 1995 was $4,000,000,000.

In 1996, handguns were used to murder 2 people in New Zealand, 15 in Japan, 30 in Great Britain, 106 in Canada and 9,390 in the United States.

In 1997, in California, there were a total of 594 firearm-related deaths for children ages 0-19. Of these deaths, 106 were suicides, 457 were homicides, 26 were accidents, and 5 were ones with unknown intent.

In 1997, homicide was the second leading cause of death among young women from ages 15 to 24.

In 1997, for every time that a civilian used a handgun to kill in self-defense, 43 people lost their lives in handgun homicides.

In 1997, the firearm injury death rate among males ages 15-24 was 42 percent higher than the motor vehicle injury death rate.

According to the Children's Defense Fund, nearly 16 children a day died in 1997 as a result of a firearms-related homicide, suicide or unintentional shooting.

In 1997 there were 15,690 homicides, of which 8,503 were committed with handguns. Only 193 (2.3 percent) handgun homicides were classified as justifiable homicides.

In 1998, over 30,000 people died from gunshots in the U.S.

In 1998, more than 10 children and teenagers ages 19 and under were killed with guns everyday.

In 1998, 30,708 people in the United States died from firearm-related deaths. 12,102 (39%) of those were murdered; 17,424 (57%) were suicides; 866 (3%) were accidents; and in 316 (1%) the intent was unknown. In comparison, 33,651 Americans were killed in the Korean War and 58,193 Americans were killed in the Vietnam War.

In 1998, gunshot wounds were the second leading cause of injury death for men and women 10-24 years of age - second only to motor vehicle crashes.

In 1998, firearm homicide was the leading cause of death for black males ages 15-34.

Gun violence is the second-leading cause of injury-related fatalities in the US after car accidents. In Alaska, Maryland and Nevada as well as D.C., firearm death rates in 1998 exceeded those for car accidents.

Comparison of U.S. gun homicides to other industrialized countries:

In 1998, handguns alone murdered:

- 373 people in Germany

- 151 people in Canada

- 57 people in Australia

- 19 people in Japan

- 54 people in England and Wales, and

- 11,789 people in the United States

- Among 26 industrialized nations, 86% of gun deaths among children under age 15 occurred in the United States.

According to the U.S. Department of Education, in 1998-99, states and territories expelled 3,523 students from bringing a firearm to school, down from 5,724 in 1996-97.

In 1999, guns in the United States murdered approximately 10,096 people. Out of all of those, there were only 154 justifiable homicides. Most young homicide victims are killed with guns. In 1999, 82 percent of homicide victims ages 15-19 were killed with firearms. Homicide is the number one cause of death among African Americans ages 15 to 24, and the second leading cause of death for Hispanics in the same age group.

In a book published in 2000, Professors Philip J. Cook and Jens Ludwig estimated that the total annual cost of gun violence in the U.S. is $100,000,000,000.

According to the Brady Campaign, in 2000, more than nine young people aged 19 and under were killed a day in gun homicides, suicides and unintentional shootings in the United States. Many more were wounded. The incidents of gun violence more frequently involve children.

Also, in 2000, 1,776 children and teenagers were murdered with guns, 1,007 committed suicide with guns, and 193 died in unintentional shootings. A total of 3,042 young people were killed by firearms in the U.S., one every three hours.

In 2000, a total of 28,663 people died from firearm injuries in the United States.

In 2000, 80% of murder victims aged 13 to 19 years old were killed with a firearm.

During 2000, 62% of all murders of those under age 18 in the U.S. involved firearms. In 1986, guns were involved in 38% of such offenses.

Of the firearm injury deaths in 2000, 62.1 percent were Caucasian males, 21.4 percent were African-American males, 11.1 percent were Caucasian females, and 2.9 percent were African-American females. The remaining 2.5 % consisted of other ethnic backgrounds.

In 2000, 3,761 American children and teens were killed by gunfire. Of these:

- 2,184 were murdered by gunfire

- 1,231 committed suicide

- 262 died from accidental shootings

- 609 were under 16 years of age

- 179 were under 10 years of age

- 83 were under 5 years of age

Americans for Gun Safety produced a 2003 report that reveals that 20 of the nation's 22 national gun laws are not enforced. According to U.S. Department of Justice data, only 2% of federal gun crimes were actually prosecuted. Eighty-five percent of cases prosecuted relate to street criminals in possession of firearms. Ignored are laws intended to punish illegal gun trafficking, firearm theft, corrupt gun dealers, lying on a criminal background check form, obliterating firearm serial numbers, selling guns to minors and possessing a gun in a school zone.

For every time a gun is used in a home in a legally justifiable shooting [note that every self-defense is legally justifiable] there are 22 criminal, unintentional, and suicide-related shootings.

Nearly 8% of adolescents in urban junior and senior high schools miss at least one day of school each month because they are afraid to attend.

In one year, more children and teens died from gunfire than from cancer, pneumonia, influenza, asthma, and HIV/AIDS combined.

Every day, more than 80 Americans die from gun violence.

The rate of firearm deaths among kids under age 15 is almost 12 times higher in the United States than in 25 other industrialized countries combined.

Firearms are the second-leading cause of death (after motor vehicle accidents) for young people 19 and under in the U.S.

The costs of treating gunshot wounds can reach over $100,000,000 at an average county hospital.

A teenager today is more likely to die from a gunshot wound than all deaths caused by disease.

According to Americans for Gun Safety, gun theft is most likely in states without laws requiring safe storage of firearms in the home and where there are large numbers of gun owners and relatively high crime rates. Based on FBI data, nearly 1.7 million guns have been reported stolen in the past ten years, and only 40% of those were recovered. The missing guns, over 80% of which are taken from homes or cars, most likely fuel the black market for criminals.

In a study of inner-city 7-year-olds and their exposure to violence, 75% of them reported hearing gunshots.

For every child killed by a gun, four are wounded.

American kids are 16 times more likely to be murdered with a gun, 11 times more likely to commit suicide with a gun, and nine times more likely to die from a firearm accident than children in 25 other industrialized countries combined.

According to a report by the Joshephson Institute of Ethics, 60% of high school and 31% of middle school boys said they could get a gun if they wanted to.

A gun kept in the home is 22 times more likely to kill a family member or a friend than it is to be used against an intruder.

On average, guns in the United States kill 10 children every day.

As high as the numbers of gun fatalities are, the number of gun-related injuries is even higher. For every firearm fatality in the United States, there are two non-fatal firearm injuries.

According to the Ohio Coalition Against Gun Violence, over 40% of American teens personally know someone who has been shot.

More than 1/3 of American teens know a teenager who has threatened to kill someone.

2/3 of students in grades 6-12 say they could obtain a firearm in 24 hours.

Nearly three times as many children under the age of 10 died from guns as the number of law enforcement officers killed in the line of duty.

Every hour in America, firearms kill four people.

A gun in your home makes it three times more likely that you or a family member will murder someone you care about.

More than one woman per day is killed with a firearm used by their husbands or intimate acquaintances during an argument.

Nonfatal injuries from gun violence are estimated to outnumber gun-related deaths by 3 to 1, meaning that there are approximately 90,000 nonfatal gun injuries each year.

Large cities claim that 72% of their school violence is attributable in part to gang activity.

According to the National Education Association, every school day, at least 100,000 students take guns to school. Also, every day, around 160,000 students do not go to school because they are afraid of being killed or injured by other students who bring guns to school. Every day, 40 students are killed or injured by firearms in school. Every day, almost 900 teachers are threatened with physical harm, and 40 of them are physically attacked.

Nearly 5,200 of the nation's secondary school teachers are physically attacked at school each month, according to the National Institute of Education. Approximately 1,000 are hurt seriously enough to require medical attention. 130,000 teachers report theft every month, and 6,000 of them have something taken from them by force.

In Chicago, it is reported that students threatened one in eleven teachers in Illinois high schools with physical harm during the month before a survey by the Criminal Justice Information Authority was taken. More than half reported that the student had used obscenity, and a third reported that a student made an obscene gesture towards them.

No religion, race, gender, or region is immune to violence in America. However, certain groups of people suffer a higher rate of violence than others. For example, in one year, 42.9% of all murders occurred in the southern states. For every 100,000 people who lived there, 11 were killed. Midwestern states accounted for 18.6% of all murders. For every 100,000 people there, seven were killed.

On average, every 1,000 teenagers experienced 67 violent crimes each year, compared to 16 for every 1,000 adults age 20 or older. Adolescents age 12 to 15 are about twice as likely as older teens to experience crimes in school. About 37% of violent crimes and 81% of crimes of theft against younger teenagers occurred at school.

Texas A&M studied 1,004 eighth and tenth grade students from 23 small Texas communities. These are the results of their study:

1) 34% of students report having been threatened with bodily harm, though not hurt, at school or on the bus. 15% of them said they had something taken from them by force or threat of bodily harm. 14% said that they had been physically attacked.

2) Half of the boys and almost 28% of the girls were in at least one fight during the previous year.

3) More than 20% said that threatening to use a weapon would help prevent fights. Nearly 17% thought that "acting tough" would deter altercations.

From a "Youth Risk Behavior Survey" conducted by the Centers for Disease Control, a sample of 11,631 students who go to school in the United States, Puerto Rico, and the Virgin Islands, 19.6% of students who were surveyed had admitted that they had carried a dangerous weapon during the previous thirty days.

A National Center for Education Statistics survey indicated that 21% of 25,000 eighth graders from 1,000 schools reported that they had witnessed weapons at school. Many students bring weapons to school because they get a sense of security.

According to the Center to Prevent Handgun Violence, over 18% of all weapons in school incidents are drug or gang-related, 15% involve long-standing disagreements, 13% involve playing with or cleaning guns, and 10% involve fights and material possessions.

In the time it took you to read this book up to this point, five people in America lost their lives to gun violence.

Bullying in Schools

School bullying has grown into a major problem in this country and around the world. Contrary to popular belief, school bullying is a major factor contributing to gun violence in our schools. It has caused the deaths of many students in our school system, and will continue to destroy our schools if no preventative action is taken.

The National Association of Elementary School Principals indicates in "Report to Parents" that one in ten students is attacked or harassed by bullies, and that 15% of school children are involved in bully/victim problems. Many other reports indicate that these statistics are obsolete, and the actual number is much larger.

According to Dr. Dan Olweus, a professor who specializes in victimization research, bullying is defined as follows: "A person is being bullied when he or she is exposed, repeatedly and over time to negative actions on the part of one or more other persons." He also says that schools across America accommodate roughly 2.1 million bullies, who harass 2.7 million victims. 3% of students in first through ninth grades are bullied at least once a week or more. While school administrators and other school staff are well aware of this problem, many just dismiss these incidents as a part of growing up.

In New York, clinical psychologist Dr. Nathaniel Floyd says that there are bullies in every state, and in every school. When graduation comes, they continue on in their old ways. If they are not stopped, these bullies will go on in life treating business partners, family members, and friends, the same way they were used to treating their victims. Many such incidents have very tragic endings. Many times, these bullies do not stop with their fists, they go on to guns and other deadly weapons, and the results are too harsh to imagine.

In Missouri, 12-year-old Nathan D. Faris went to DeKalb High School. Every day, Nathan attended school, and was taunted as being "chubby", a "walking dictionary", and "fat". 12-year-old Benji Chapman said of him, "It's been happening ever since the third or fourth grade. People teased him because he wore sunglasses. They called him 'Sunny'- for that, and also because he's fat."

On a Monday in March 1987, just as classes had begun, Nathan pulled a pistol out of a duffel bag and started pointing it around the classroom. Many other students began to taunt him, and doubted the gun was real. A classmate, Timothy Perrin, age 13, jumped up and grabbed Nathan's wrists, trying to get him top let go. He thought it was fake, so he gave up and returned to his seat, laughing. Nathan fired a shot at Tim, but missed. Students screamed in shock and horror as they came to grips with the reality of the situation. The gun they originally believed to be phony was actually real. They were all in serious danger of getting hurt, or even killed.

Seventh graders ran from the social studies classroom in fear of being shot. Nathan fired more shots at the students. He wounded Timothy, who then staggered out of the room. Nathan then shot himself in the head. Timothy was fortunate, and survived. Nathan, however, did not.

As we reflect on this case, and many similar incidents around this country, we must ask ourselves what was really going on inside Nathan Faris's head. Nathan had been taunted daily; he had been laughed at, made fun of, and harassed on a regular basis. He had bottled up inside himself the anger and frustration he had felt every time someone laughed at him, called him fat, or teased him. His feelings were closed to all but himself, until one day he decided to take the cap off of the bottle containing his feelings.

This incident, and many others like it, could have been prevented, had there been policies in the school that gave significant punishments to all harassers and bullies. It is not right for an educator to say that bullying is part of growing up. The problem is that it should not have to be a part of growing up, and if this problem is dealt with, it won't be.

When you consider what a bully truly is, you will see that they all contain similar characteristics. They are always quick to start a fight, and they often use tactics of intimidation, force, and aggressiveness. They also enjoy dominating over other children. Bullies also make threats, call students names, and shout insults. For these reasons and others, they often stand out in their class.

According to a 22-year study, a class bully who terrorizes his/her classmates has a one in four chance of having a criminal record by the age of thirty. Those children who are not school bullies have a one in twenty chance of becoming a criminal. Leonard Eron and other psychologists traced 870 third graders from Columbia County, New York, and analyzed them by their family, what they saw on television, and other factors. The children who were the most aggressive were most likely to drop out of school and get in trouble with the law as teenagers.

Of the 409 children who were found at age 30, those who had been bullies as children tended to have children who were bullies. They have also been found to punish their children severely, abuse their wives, and be convicted for violent crimes.

Many childhood bullies were abused when they grew up, and they saw their parents physically fight, or abuse their siblings. The transformation of normal children to bullies occurs because they think that violence is an appropriate means to achieve their goals. Bullies are often children abused by their parents, who discipline their children severely; as a result, the children come to believe that violence is acceptable. Harvard psychologist Dr. Ronald Slaby says that parents teach their children to strike back at the least incitement.

According to the National Association of School Psychologists, the number of bullies and their victims range from between 15% and 30% of the student body. A study also found that direct, physical bullying increases during elementary school years, peaks in middle school, and drops during high school. However, verbal abuse remains constant throughout the school years.

The victims of all bullies have similar characteristics. They are smaller or weaker than the bullies. They are usually overweight, wear glasses, or have some unusual physical characteristics. Children who are bullied have a shrinking self-confidence. Their feelings about themselves change dramatically, almost to the point where they believe they deserve to be beaten up. Some victims, like some abusers, are abused in their own home.

According to Dr. Olweus, bullying is a growing problem. After working at Stanford University, he published his discoveries, and advised numerous recommendations that would be applicable in schools. Some of these recommendations include:

- Making sure that there is always adult supervision at recess.

- Creating non-physical punishments to abusive or misbehaving children.

- Practicing severe enforcement of the rules of behavior.

- Children should be encouraged to gain and maintain good friends.

- Develop a curriculum that promotes communication, friendship and assertive skills, teaches anger management and conflict resolution, and includes lessons about bullying.

Today there are several school districts in the United States that have programs that deal with school bullying. In southern Westchester County, New York, Dr. Nathaniel Floyd started an anti-bullying program. In this program, bullies are counseled individually and in groups. They are taught that there is a need to gain control over the need to bully. According to Dr. Floyd, the most effective strategy for victims is not to fight aggressively. Instead, it is encouraged that they stand with dignity.

PART III:

THE MEDIA AND ITS IMPACT ON CHILDREN

TELEVISION AND BEHAVIOR IN CHILDREN

Television and the media in general, are factors that have been linked to violence in children. The scenes that many children see on TV create a huge impression on them, and drive many of them to violent actions. Consider the following:

A five-year-old watches an episode of Superman. Later that day, he decides to play Superman, and jumps out the window. He dies instantly.

A nine-year-old watches an action movie and decides to play James Bond. He takes out a gun his parents hid for protection, and shoots himself in the head.

A nine-year-old watches wrestling with his friend. He decides to mimic the wrestler, and pull some wrestling stunts on his friend. He severely injures his friend, who later dies.

In a very famous case, Omar Soto, a ten-year-old, was watching the movie Gotcha with his friend. After watching scenes where college students played with fake guns, Omar's friend went home to get some real guns. He returned with three guns, one of which was a .357 magnum. When he tried to cock the gun, it fired, and shot Omar in the head, killing him.

Examining these and hundreds of other such cases may make you believe that the media is largely responsible for gun-related deaths among minors. This theory is incorrect. However, the media's regular display of violence certainly contributes to gun-related deaths among children. At the same time, it is not the only factor of such deaths, but one of many.

When examining the violence in today's media, one must look at what today's children watch. Some children watch outrageous programming containing graphic violence, which even many adults would find obscene. The pictures of blood, gore, and mutilation are enough to make one's mind spin. What impact does that have on a child's mind? Researchers believe it has many.

When movies or television shows label "good guys" and "bad guys", viewers are led to believe that the violence committed by the "good guys" is acceptable and understandable in any situation. Since the media shows that "good guys" are the heroes and would never do anything wrong, younger viewers, who are more impressionable than older people, may be led to believe that shooting people is acceptable, provided you are on the "good" side.

Another impact made on younger viewers is that when weapons are used, no one gets hurt. This assumption is brought on by the fact that one person gets shot and falls to the ground. However, at the end of the movie, he is alive and well. There have been movies where a character gets shot, stabbed, kicked, punched, and beaten with a pole, yet throughout the movie he seems to be in reasonable health.

Of course, for all of us who realize that the fighting, shooting, and beating aren't real, the movie seems acceptable. The blood is artificial, as are all the injuries received. Older people realize that these "victims" are really actors, and none of them were injured in the least bit throughout the creation of the film. Imagine if you will, that someone gets shot, stabbed, stepped on, and beaten. This man also suffers from broken bones and internal bleeding. Then, he runs out of a building that has caught fire, carrying a person to safety just before the building collapses. Can you imagine that he is still able to walk around, and appear to be in decent shape? Not likely.

However, for younger viewers, these scenes create an image that all people are indestructible, and cannot be hurt. Therefore, they find it perfectly acceptable to do harm to other children, and believe that these children will be unharmed. It is not so far-fetched for them to believe that the person they shoot will be unhurt, that the person they maimed will be alive, and that the skin they stab with a knife will draw no real blood. These images and ideas, implanted into their mind by the media, continue to grow until children take deadly actions.

These deadly actions are caused by the media's graphic violence on films or regular TV shows. Some shows even promote guns, displaying them on TV like trophies, ready to be used and enjoyed. Allowing such programs on television create an insecurity for parents. Parents who want to shield their children to such graphic violence cannot leave their children alone to watch TV.

While 40 years ago, most television programs may have been acceptable; today's quality of television programming is abhorrent to many. The worst thing ever displayed on television in the 1960's is today's best programming. The point is not to degrade the culture for what it has become, but to explain the impact it has had on younger viewers. Television producers and network owners are not interested in the quality of the television programming shown today, rather they are more concerned with their ratings. If ratings go up, whatever they have shown will be shown again. Whatever creates bigger capital and greater funding for their network, will be shown ad nauseam.

Movies are not the only source for the graphic violence that is fed to younger viewers. Even a perfunctory glance at the news today will demonstrate the media's fascination with violence. Seemingly endless coverage of wars, genocides, and even local shootings, all show younger people the rampant bloodshed that exists in today's world. While sheltering children from reality may certainly be harmful, it is important for parents to find a balance between the truths their children need to see, and the violence they don't.

Over the past 15 years, the news media has shown an increasing amount of violence on television. Whether it is covering a war, a natural disaster, or all too common crimes and murders, newscasts have become a constant source of violence and gore, displaying these scenes repeatedly in the ever-demanding 24-hour news cycle. Today, the news networks must compete with the regular networks for viewers, and so they create programming that would appeal to most people who are somewhat interested in the news of the day. By providing scenes that capture viewers' attention, the networks are able to stay on top, and continue to exist.

As a result, news programs, which were once used for the purposes of gathering information, have become like most other media sources- presenting scenes appealing to people with little or no informational or educational benefit. The problem presents itself when a child innocently decides to watch a news program for a school project, or out of sheer interest in the news of the day. When he or she is bombarded with the images of violence, the child can become confused as to what can be considered appropriate violence, or for that matter, if there is even an inappropriate violence, and casts doubt on those who oppose media violence on the basis of his or reliance on the ethics and integrity of the news media.

There is little wrong with a 26-year-old man who understands that what he is watching is fake, to watch a violent movie or newscast. There is certainly something wrong, however, with a six-year-old boy, who does not share a similar understanding of what really went on during the creation of the film or TV show, to watch that same show. The impression the child is left with after watching that movie is far more extreme than the impression left with the adult after watching the same program.

A study by the American Psychological Association found that children who watch more violent programs than other children are less likely to call for help when violent actions take place, such as fights, etc. They also found that in general, children who continuously watch violence on television are less sensitive to the pain and suffering of others. Additionally, they may become more fearful of the world around them, or believe that the world is a dangerous place.

In a study done at Pennsylvania State University, about 100 preschoolers were observed before and after watching television. Some children were shown cartoons with no violence, and others were shown cartoons with a lot of violence. Those who were shown the violent cartoons were more likely to argue and use violence as a means to achieve their goals; for example, by hitting their friends. They were also found to disobey rules more often, and leave tasks unfinished, and display a greater sense of impatience.

In 2002, CBS News reported the results of a study that followed seven hundred people from various backgrounds, from when they were fourteen through thirty. The study found that there was a link between those who watched one hour of television a day, and incidents of violence. This study concretely proved a direct link between watching television and committing acts of violence.

Other studies found long-term consequences of watching violence on television. A study of elementary school children found that those who watched violence as a child became violent teenagers. Additionally, by the time they were 30, those who watched more TV were more likely to be arrested, and have a criminal record as adults.

Under the current law, networks are not responsible for things that occur as a result of their programming; it is the parent's responsibility to have control over the programs their children watch. Of course, this is not legally mandatory. If any parent wishes to let his/her child to watch whatever the child wants to watch, that is their preroga-tive. However, any violent actions taken by that child sub-sequent to his/her viewing of the TV show or movie are at least partially the responsibility of the child's parents.

Technological advances made in the field of TV locks and ratings have made it easier for parents to leave their chil-dren alone in front of the television, knowing that noth-ing that they don't want their children to see will be seen. TV ratings, such as TV-G, TV-PG, TV-14, and TV-MA, make it clear as to what audience the program is geared towards. Additional ratings, such as L for language, or V for violence, also notify viewers as to what the program may contain.

The V-CHIP, which is available to all, can block out any programming that parents may not want their children to see. Therefore, it is now easier for parents to feel more secure about what their children are watching. Additional locks that are offered through cable networks make it even easier for parents to let their children watch TV.

There are other things that parents can do to ensure the protection of their children from offensive programming. Watching at least one episode of a show before allowing their child to do the same, will give a parent a better idea of what the show contains, and they can restrict their chil-dren from watching that show in the future. Furthermore, watching a violent program with your children once, and afterwards discussing the violence that the child saw, may help as well. Parents should make it clear that the violence on the show was not real, and real violence is unaccept-able. By making children aware of other avenues of solv-ing problems, such as talking to others or asking for help, parents can minimize the amount of violence their child sees and commits.

Although many may argue, it is believed that violence in the media is a major cause of youth violence. While this may be largely untrue, it is true that when children watch movies such as the Terminator movies, True Lies, Die Hard, or the many other action movies that contain graphic violence, they are left with a feeling that violence is common and even tolerable, in certain situations.

Of course, it is wrong to think that violence is acceptable. But is it only the media that produces a trigger reaction in a young child's mind, causing them to commit unthinkable acts? Or is it something else? Maybe science may never tell us what generates violent reactions in children. Maybe it is a combination of many different events in a child's life, which lead a child to act in a certain way. Maybe it is something simpler than any of us might have ever imagined. But whatever it is, we must find it, and put an end to it.

Video Games and Behavior in Children

There is another factor that many believe causes violent behavior among children. This is something that children are involved with all the time- video games. Whether on the computer, or on game systems, such as Nintendo[64], Play Station, Microsoft X Box, or PS2, most of the games played are a lot of fun, and children can play with it for hours. The graphics and the realistic sights and sounds make it more insidious and alluring to younger people. However, the games that are currently being marketed to children are as violent as ever. Besides the typical killings, the graphics shown are immeasurably sordid.

What makes video games more despicable than violent television is the active part children take in the killings. Children can hold a gun (not a real gun, but a model of a gun that resembles a real one), and fire at people on the screen. These games, along with others, get children riled up about killing people the same way they kill the characters in their game. Other games allow players to kill and urinate on police officers, and beat women to death to get their money.

While these games may be enjoyable to many, most are only suitable for older people, or those who understand that what they are watching is not real, and will not respond violently after playing that game.

When a parent gives his/her child a video game system, it is like giving their child a license to commit acts of violence. When the child plays the game, the impression made on their young minds is the worst that can possibly be made; far worse than watching any violent TV show. When you give a child a violent video game, you are basically teaching them how to be violent and use weapons effectively. You are teaching them how to inflict the maximum amount of damage you can on another person.

The Entertainment Software Rating Board (ESRB) has issued ratings for video games. These ratings include: EC- for those in early childhood, E- for everyone, T- for teens 13 and older, M- for mature players, and AO- for adults only. Many critics of the ESRB claim that the Boards ratings underestimate the content of the game. 70% of all games are rated E. Almost all games contain some form of violence, and most of those have extremely graphic violence.

Games that include people getting run over by cars, or meeting similar violent ends, are marketed specifically to younger audiences. For example, in an older game, Carmageddon 2: Carpocalypse Now, the victim in the game gets run over by the players car, and his blood is splattered all over the car and road. If you want, you can make him commit suicide, and if you're in a particularly gory mood, you can dismember him as well.

Perhaps one of the most infamous violent video games ever created was Grand Theft Auto. In 2002, the first edition of Grand Theft Auto came out, called "Vice City". That was based on a city similar to Miami in the 1980's. In 2004, the creators of Grand Theft Auto came out with a sequel, entitled "Grand Theft Auto: San Andreas". In this game, the player controls 'CJ', someone who decided to join gangs to avenge the death of his mother. Activities in this game include driving and shooting through a city, being able to carjack any car you see, and getting chased by the police, and shooting back. The player can also perform missions like killing mob bosses, hijacking trains, and excelling in hand-to-hand combat.

In the summer of 2003, near the town of Newport, Tennessee, William Buckner, 16, and his step-brother Joshua, 13, were playing "Grand Theft Auto: Vice City". After they finished playing, they decided to have a little more fun by acting out the scenes from the game. They took two rifles, left their home, and hid in trees along a highway. As cars went by, the two boys began to shoot at them. When they were finished, they had killed a man, and critically injured a woman.

In another game, "25 to Life", the player gets chased by police, shoots back at them, and also uses humans as shields to protect themselves. In response, U.S. Senator Chuck Schumer (D-NY), said, "It's the worst in a series of violent and gruesome games that lower the common denominator of decency."

These and hundreds of other games that contain extreme violence are marketed towards younger players. Once again, it is acceptable for someone who understands the concept of a game- that it is inherently unrealistic, to play the game. People have the right to market these games, but they should not be marketed to children. The sale of an extremely violent video game to a child is analogous to the sale of cigarettes, alcohol, or guns, to a minor.

When the program known as 'We Card' began, no more minors were able to purchase cigarettes. The 'We Card' program was put into place because cigarettes are harmful to people, and in order to reduce the rate of teen smoking, people were no longer able to buy them without proper ID. This resulted in keeping minors safe from physical harm, by making it almost impossible for them to get a hold of cigarettes.

Violent video games are harmful as well, both physically and mentally. They are harmful physically, because a child who plays such video games will be tempted to attempt the things they do on the video game at home or in school. So it is physically dangerous, not only to the buyer, but also to others as well, just as cigarettes present a danger to others from the second hand smoke it emits.

It is mentally harmful as well, since while playing those video games, children get the idea that such violence is acceptable. Such thoughts may increase as time goes by, until that child takes violent action.

A group called Mothers Against Videogame Addiction And Violence (MAVAV), has come out with a myriad of facts and warning signs to help parents detect Videogame Addiction and their effects in children. They say that videogame addiction can hinder the development of social skills among children, and also burden many children with sadness and depression in their life. A way you can tell if your child is addicted to video games, they say, is to check his/her report card. If a child excels in Computer Education, but is doing poor in English, Math, Science, Social Studies, Physical Education, or any other academic subject, it could indicate that the child is a "troubled video game player".

Another genre of video games is the Massive Multiplayer Online Role Playing Game (MMORPG). This is the kind of video game where people take on roles of other people. People with low self-esteem who seek an escape from their everyday life too often abuse these games. It often leads to anxiety, depression, loss of interest in everyday life, and sleeplessness. Many compare it to alcohol or drug dependency.

Stores should not sell games that are too violent for some, based on the age of the buyer. The following chart is a result of a compilation of reports and research that have suggestions as to which games may be appropriate to which age groups, based on the ESRB rating system:

AGE	EC	E	T	M	AO
3-6	YES	NO	NO	NO	NO
7-12	YES	YES	NO	NO	NO
13-17	YES	YES	YES	NO	NO
18-20	YES	YES	YES	YES	NO
21 +	YES	YES	YES	YES	YES

If we start implementing small reforms like that, we may reduce the number of deaths among young people caused by the images that children see when playing video games. Violent images create long-lasting impressions that influence the actions a person will take.

It is small things that add up to actions a person may take, and we must do all we can to suppress feelings of violence among children and teenagers. We must take actions to prevent violence in our homes, our communities, and in our nation. Any action, no matter how insignificant it may seem, like restricting the sale of certain video games to children, will help immensely.

Children need direction with which to learn and grow. Selling obscenely violent video games to them will show them that they are allowed to see and be involved in the violent situations they find themselves on video games. Their rationalization may be correct, since the adults they trust to watch over and protect them are allowing them to play violent games. If adults give them these games, they reason that it is acceptable to react violently in real life, since such reactions are displayed in their games.

Parents must also make sure that these children don't visit friends who have such games. Although, just like television, video games are not the primary cause of violence in children, they are one of many causes. Therefore, we must protect them from these and all other negative influences, no matter the cost.

Violent Music and Behavior in Children

It has been argued that violent music brings about violent behavior in children, especially teenagers. Since the beginning of the 1980's, many people began to get angry over the lyrics of pop music, and many organizations were formed to target artists and record labels that produce such music. Many organizations testified before Congress about atrocities that occurred after young people listened to punk rock and rap.

Such organizations, many of which exist today, compare record companies to tobacco companies. They do so because they believe that tobacco companies target young people as customers for two reasons- younger people are more impressionable, and also the tobacco industry will then have a customer for life, since tobacco is addictive. So too, they believe, record companies target younger audiences with violent songs for the same reasons, and this leads to violent reactions by children.

Many young people have confirmed that the message in rap is clear, and in the words of one teen, "killing people and being on death row is cool."

Today's rap is rampant with messages of violence, drugs, racism, and the debasing of women. Rap artists continue to harp on these images, explicitly describing horrific acts of violence, racist attitudes, and perverse themes, in an attempt to be more successful than their competitors. This competition has led them to be more explicit and violent with every album they put out.

According to Mediascope, an informational research group, teenagers spend between 4 and 5 hours a day listening to music and watching music videos. 48% of Americans say that violence in popular music should be more heavily regulated, and 59% would like to restrict violence in music. 47% of mothers with children in public schools believe that violent messages in rap music contribute "a great deal" to school violence, and 66% of 13- to 17-year-olds believe that violence in music is partly responsible for violent crimes.

Here are some excerpts from various artists:

Notorious BIG - Come On

I shot dread in the head, took the bread and the landspread
Lil' Gotti got the shotty to your body
So don't resist, or you might miss Christmas
I tote guns, I make number runs
I give emcees the runs drippin
When I throw my clip in the AK, I slay from far away
Everybody hit the DECK.

(From Born Again, released posthumously, Bad Boy
Entertainment 1999)

Snoop Dogg - 20 Dollars 2 My Name

Nothing left to do, but buy some shells for my glock
Why? so I can rob every known dope spot
I got 19 dollars and 50 cents up in my pocket with what?
With this automatic rocket
Gotta have it to pop it, unlock it, and take me up a hostage.
(From Da Game Is To Be Sold, Not To Be Told, Priority
Records 1998)

Tha Eastsidaz - Another Day

How much dirt have I done
My life has just begun
I sleep with my gun
My problems weigh a ton...
Live by the gun die by the gun.
(From Snoop Dogg Presents The Eastsidaz, Doggystyle
Records, 2000)

2Pac - Five Deadly Venomz

I got a glock that say 'Pac run the block...
My gauge gets me... PAID
As I sit and reminisce about the old days
Hugging on my AK... getting played, hey ...
I pop a clip and grip my nine tight
Now it's on everyday could be my last day
That's why I blast on they a-- as I past let the glass spray.
(Interscope 1993)

Outkast - Ain't No Thang

I'd do it if I have to
Bustin caps with this a heat and load it clip up after clip
I'm packin my gauge, if I feel it
The glock, the gat, the nine, the heaters
See I be bustin caps like my amp be bustin speakers
So how do you figure that Big Boi be scared to blast ya
You 'posed to be quickest draw, but man, I hail em faster
1-2-3, you need to think about the future
Before I shoot you're a-- and dilute your blood with lead
From my hollow tips, I'll send you to an early grave.
(From Southernplayalisticadillacmuzik, La Face 1994)

Ludacris - Cry Babies (Oh No)

I caught him with a blow to the chest
My hollow put a hole in his vest
I'm bout to send two to his dome
Cry babies go home!
I just bought some new guns my mama said "it ain't
worth it"
But I'm at the shooting range just cause
Practice makes perfect.
(From Word of Mouf, Defjam, 2001)

Big Pun - Brave In The Heart

I'm from where the guns love to introduce theyself
Reduce your health, little bulletproofs get felt
Make way for krill, I don't play I spray for real
Blow your top with the glock, that's my favorite kill
Blaze your crib with like thirty shots
I'm already hot, but my last one is with some dirty cops
Blow a hole through your ribs just for runnin your lips

The street's a trip; either you deep or you sleep with the fish.
(from Endangered Species, released posthumously, Loud
2001)

C-Murder - Constantly 'N Danger

Bulletproof vest on my chest
And bulletproof windshields to catch the rest...
My money bigger, huh, so I got a bigger gun too
I keep a nine with me, if you want me come get me
You shoot first... you better hit me
I keep a close eye on a stranger...
Cause I'm constantly in danger .
(From Life or Death, Priority 1998)

Tupac Shakur - Bury Me A G

I got nothin' to lose sos I choose to be a killer
Went from bangin to slangin
Now I'm a dope dealer
All my a paid the price to be a boss
Backin school
Wrote the rules on gettin' tossed
Popping rocks on the block was a past time
Pack a 9 all the time.
(From Thug Life, Jive 1998)

Eminem- Bad Influence

I'm the illest rapper to hold the cordless, patrollin corners
Looking for hookers to punch in the mouth with a roll
of quarters.....
You probably think that I'm a negative person, don't be

so sure of it
I don't promote violence, I just encourage it.
(Platinum Collection 2001)

On March 24, 1998, in Jonesboro, Arkansas, Mitchell Johnson and Andrew Golden killed four students and a teacher, and injured many more during their shooting rampage at their school. It is now believed that Mitchell Johnson may have been influenced by rap music prior to the shooting.

Only a few months before the shooting, around Christmas time, Mitchell bought some rap tapes with the money he received as a Christmas present from a relative. Among those tapes were albums by TuPac Shakur, and Bone Thugs N Harmony. When classes resumed, students realized a change in Mitchell's behavior. He started making gang signs around the school, and his whole demeanor changed.

Once a quiet, friendly, never hostile student, Mitchell Johnson changed after being tainted by the lyrics of rap. He exhibited signs of violence, like the gang sign on the cover of TuPac's album, All Eyez On Me. After the shooting incident, Mitchell himself said that the music may have influenced him to do what he did because that kind of music can draw a person in.

Surveys of three middle schools at the time, one in Arkansas and one in Missouri, indicated that a large percentage of students listened to rap. 39% to 84% of students listened to TuPac, and 37% to 84% listened to Bone Thugs. These are the results of the surveys taken:

- First School: 7th graders- 39% listen to TuPac, and 67% to Bone Thugs.

- Second School: 8th graders- 68% listen to TuPac, and 84% to Bone Thugs.

- Third School: 9th graders- 82% listen to TuPac, and 37% to Bone Thugs.

In Missouri, the survey was conducted in the 5th, 6th, 7th, and 8th grades. Here are the results:

- 5th Grade- 65% to TuPac and 77% to Bone Thugs.

- 6th Grade- 65% to TuPac and 75% to Bone Thugs.

- 7th and 8th Grade- 58% to TuPac and 78% to Bone Thugs.

Music videos have an even greater effect on the minds of its young viewers. Many believe that the lyrics' potential impact is magnified by the accompanying video images. In it's efforts to uncover the effects of music videos, Mediascope cited a 1996 study that revealed that boys and girls ages 12 to 19 watch MTV for an average of 6.6 and 6.2 hours each week, respectively. A 1998-1999 study revealed that music videos were more violent than feature films and television, averaging four violent scenes each, and a 1997 study reported that 22.4% of MTV videos contained overt violence, and 25% depicted weapon carrying.

The American Academy of Pediatrics reported that portrayals of violence in popular music videos could distort adolescents' expectations about conflict resolution, race, and male-female relationships. In a 1998 study of 518 music videos from the four most popular music video networks, almost 15% contained interpersonal violence, averaging 6 violent acts per violence-containing video. Males and females were equally portrayed as victims of violence, but men were three times as likely to be the aggressors and white females were most frequently the victims. African Americans were also overrepresented as both aggressors and victims and were 28 times more likely to be portrayed as victims of violence than aggressors.

In the 1980's, the nonprofit organization known as the Parent's Music Resource Center, or PMRC, was formed. This organization called for all music albums to be rated in one of four categories, depending on the song's explicit lyrics. The organization also wanted songs with offensive lyrics not to be displayed on album covers.

Soon, the PMRC enrolled Jeff Ling, a rock musician, to narrate a slide show at a church in Washington. 350 people attended this slide show, which warned parents of the offensive lyrics in rock songs that were available to their children. Among the 350 visitors was the wife of Eddie Frits, the president of the National Association of Broadcasters. He had written to the heads of many recording companies asking that copies of lyrics accompany all recordings made available to broadcasters. The point was that if any offensive lyrics were heard in those songs, broadcasters would not play those songs. Many heads of recording companies cried foul. "It smells of censorship," one complained.

One of the founders of the PMRC was Tipper Gore, wife of then Senator Al Gore. She was horrified at the lyrics of songs, and decided to help form the PMRC. In September of 1985, she testified in front of the Commerce, Science, and Transportation Committee, headed by John Danforth. Al Gore, Jr., who was already planning to run for president in 1988, supported his wife's claim slightly less in Congress than in private. This was because he knew that Hollywood had long been an enormous source of money for campaigns.

Many other Senators were also afraid to offend the companies who filled their campaign war chests. The Chairman, John Danforth, began by noting that even though the music "glorifies violence in various forms, I do not know of any suggestion that any legislation be passed." Senator James Exon of Nebraska wondered about the purpose of having such a meeting when no legislation would be passed on the issue.

The cowardice of the Senate was so pervasive through the hearings, that many considered it humorous. One respected member of the Senate, however, saw nothing funny about it. Senator Fritz Hollings referred to the lyrics as "outrageous filth" and remarked, "If I could find some way constitutionally to do away with it, I would."

Rock star Frank Zappa told the committee, "The PMRC proposal is an ill-conceived piece of nonsense, which... infringes on the civil liberties of people." Zappa called PMRC "a cult", and its members, "cultural terrorists". He also asked the committee: "Is it proper that the husband of a PMRC founder sits on any committee considering business pertaining to...his wife's lobbying organization? Can any committee thus constituted find facts in a fair and unbiased manner?"

Gore's response to Zappa's savage accusations of his wife was mild. He told Zappa he was a fan of his music, and that "the PMRC says repeatedly no legislation, no regulation, no government action."

While many Senators were restrained in their accusations, the organizations set up to attack the record companies did not let up. They continued to berate record companies, and will, for years to come.

Unfortunately, the debates on violent music never go anywhere. Congress cannot enact a bill that would take away the First Amendment rights of the recording companies to sell the lyrics that bring many juveniles to commit heinous crimes. Many believe that the government has no control over what songs are sold in the United States. Congress, for sure, will not allow violent songs to be banned from stores, or from being shown on television.

Many public officials believe that it is a parent's responsibility to censor what their child hears, and if they don't censor what their children hear, neither the record companies nor Congress can be held responsible for the actions taken by the children who listen to such music.

So while no laws can really be made against the sale of violent music, we can only use our own sense, and follow the old axiom: buyer beware.

PART IV:

THE LEGAL BATTLE

THE SECOND AMENDMENT: PART I: OPPOSITION TO GUN CONTROL

"A WELL REGULATED MILITIA, BEING NECESSARY TO THE SECURITY OF A FREE STATE, THE RIGHT OF THE PEOPLE TO KEEP AND BEAR ARMS, SHALL NOT BE INFRINGED."

To understand the meaning of these words, which compose our Second Amendment, one must understand the legal process of defining the true meaning of our Constitution, and the intention of its framers.

Our government is made up of three branches: Executive, Legislative, and Judicial. Each branch has checks and balances against the others. In the realm of laws, the legislative branch (Congress) passes laws, and the president chooses to sign them into law or not. The president is elected to enforce those laws, and can choose to propose laws that the Congress votes on. The Judicial branch can decide whether or not the laws are Constitutional, a right given to them by the Marbury v. Madison decision rendered by the Court in 1803.

Regardless of any opinion one might have, on this or any other issue, the Courts decide the interpretation of our laws and our Constitution. Congress cannot legalize any measure without the approval of the Court, but Congress does have the power to confirm or deny any appointment that the President makes to the Courts. Our system was designed to ensure that all three branches had equal say in the laws, and they did that by charging each branch with a different role in the process: The legislature proposes and votes on bills, the president signs and enforces those laws, and the judiciary decides their Constitutionality.

In the gun control debate, much of the argument of the gun rights organizations is the wording of the Second Amendment to the Constitution; "the right of the people to keep and bear arms, shall not be infringed". The true meaning of those words has been the center of debate from the moment they were written. Many explanations have been given by both sides to support their arguments. Using the same words, each side of the debate seems to believe the Second Amendment clearly espouses their ideology.

In truth, we may never know exactly what the Founding Fathers meant when they ratified the Second Amendment. Most likely, they would agree with different points from both sides, but we may never really know their exact beliefs. What we do know is that we must gain a clearer understanding of the practical applications of the Second Amendment in the context of today's society.

In 1791, the Founding Fathers wrote these words, and ratified them into law as the Second Amendment to the

United States Constitution. These words, while seemingly straightforward, have caused a controversy that has lasted for many years. The exact interpretation of these words implies that all people are allowed, under law, to own a firearm. Many others, however, interpret these words to mean that guns are not allowed to everyone, only to a select few.

The Americans who oppose gun control say that the words, "the right of the people to keep and bear arms shall not be infringed" imply that all people have the right to own firearms. They argue that the Founding Fathers would allow any citizen, at any time, for any reason, to own a firearm. This, they say, is because the Founding Fathers made the law specifically to prevent any future leader of this country to take away the citizen's rights to own and use guns.

It is also contended that owning a gun is absolutely necessary for personal security and well being in today's era of violence and crime. Many gun-rights activists say that it is not the millions of people who own guns that are responsible for gun violence. They substantiate their claim by showing studies that confirm that 99% of legal gun owners do not commit crimes with their guns, and all the violence comes from those who have abusive backgrounds.

Therefore, gun rights activists believe, the problem is not legal gun owners; it is the criminals who misuse them. Therefore, they say, the solution is not to control the legal ownership of guns, rather there must be stricter enforcement of the laws, and greater punishment for those who break them. Several recommended ways of doing this are putting more police officers on the streets, giving harsher, more severe punishments for crime, and providing counselors to troubled teens and others across the country.

Several national organizations have made it their duty to make sure that no gun control laws ever pass on the local, state, and federal levels. Ranking high among these organizations are the Citizens Committee for the Right To Keep and Bear Arms, Gun Owners of America, the Second Amendment Foundation, and the NRA (National Rifle Association).

The Citizens Committee for the Right to Keep and Bear Arms is an organization committed to preserving individuals' rights to gun ownership. They conduct research projects and seminars about gun control legislation. They also have a Political Action Committee committed to supporting candidates for public office that oppose gun control. They have a monthly newsletter distributed to its members, and also hold an annual conference.

The Second Amendment Foundation focuses on doing research on the meaning and significance of the Second Amendment. It does not lobby at all; rather, it seeks to educate gun owners about the meaning of the Second Amendment, and the current issues revolving around it. It fiercely opposes gun control, and urges its members to become more aware about gun control proposals, and oppose them as well.

Another pro-gun organization, Firearms And Liberty, presents this claim on their website as evidence of the need for guns, and the supposed foolishness of gun control:

> "700,000 U.S. physicians cause over 120,000 accidental deaths per year.
> There are over 80,000,000 U.S. firearm owners.
> Number of accidental deaths?

1,500 in all age groups.
Statistically speaking…
Doctors are 9,000 times more dangerous than gun
owners."

Of all the groups mentioned above, the greatest organization by far is the National Rifle Association. They say that their primary goal is to uphold the right of all people to own firearms. They will defeat any legislation that will, in their words, "deprive citizens of their rights to purchase, own, or use firearms for legitimate sporting and defensive purposes."

The NRA publishes a monthly newsletter that tells its readers when new gun legislation is going to Congress, and warns them to tell their legislators not to support any of them. They also try to manipulate people by telling them of miraculous stories about how guns save the lives of their owners. In short, they try to demonstrate to the country that gun control is bad.

The NRA has a membership of over 3 million. Many say they have joined out of their fear of violence. They also say that they just want their fundamental, constitutional right to own a gun and defend themselves. They argue that legitimate, experienced hunters pose no threat and should not have their right to hunt violated.

When discussing the Second Amendment, many contend that the word "militia" in the Second Amendment does not apply just to military forces. Therefore, an individual's right to gun ownership is not restricted under the Second Amendment. Anti gun control activists feel that when the Second Amendment says, "the right of the people to keep and bear arms shall not be infringed", it means that there is an unconditional right for all individuals to own a gun. They believe that there is no connection between the right to keep and bear arms and the presence of a well-regulated militia.

They also believe that the phrase "well regulated militia" implies that there is some sort of authority over the militia, and since the Founding Fathers wanted civilian control over the military, it appears that they support an individual's right to own guns as well. They also believe that since a well-regulated militia is necessary to the security of a free state, "the right to keep and bear arms shall not be infringed" against those individuals who own guns for protection.

As for why the Second Amendment mentions militias at all, anti gun control advocates claim that the right of an individual to own a gun was always a pre-assumed right. The sole purpose of the Second Amendment, they say, is that it guarantees that the right of the militias to use guns is a constitutional one, and that right is universal to all Americans.

There are many loopholes in the Second Amendment that can be used to bolster both sides of the gun control debate. The vague language the Founding Fathers used cannot definitively prove one way or another. Rather, it is up to us, the descendants of these great people, to discern their true intentions.

PART II:
ADVOCACY FOR GUN CONTROL

Those who support gun control believe that gun ownership is not an absolute right- it is a right that is only guaranteed for all provided that it is safe for the general public. They validate this idea by citing two phrases in the Second Amendment: "the right of the people to keep and bear Arms", and "a well-regulated militia."

The statement "a well-regulated militia" was meant to prevent the federal government from interfering with the rights of the states by meddling with their militia. This is interpreted to mean that owning a gun is not something everyone can do; it is a privilege restricted to the militia. According to the Brady Campaign, the word "militia" did not refer to the people at large, like the NRA says. "Indeed, membership in the 18th century militia was generally limited to able-bodied white males between the ages of 18 and 45 - hardly encompassing the entire population of the nation."

The statement "the right of the people to keep and bear arms" can be explained to mean that when the people as a whole are protecting themselves, they can own guns. This does not mean that any individual can own guns.

An example of this type of ownership is the minutemen in the Revolutionary War. They were a group of people who would be ready in a minute (hence "minutemen"), when the British would come. They were an example of the term "people" stated in the Second Amendment.

It is also worthy to note that at the time the Second Amendment was written, the ownership of a gun by an individual was a vital ingredient to their security and well-being. Certainly, the Founding Fathers would never have imagined that this country would suffer the way it is suffering today.

- Between 1,000 and 2,000 fatal accidental shootings, and between 15,000 and 16,000 gun suicides annually.

- Thousands of drive-by shootings annually.

- Thousands of car hijackings.

- Increasing drug consumption.

- Gang warfare over the sales of drugs.

- Rampant school shootings.

- Increased security in preschools to ensure that a four-year-old does not bring a pistol to school.

Polls indicate that Americans increasingly favor the enactment of strict gun control measures. Despite this, organizations such as the NRA oppose the ratification of even the slightest gun control measure, such as the Brady Bill. Gun lobbyists believe that the law strictly allows them to own their own firearms, no matter the cost in lives.

Despite what the NRA feels, gun control is necessary because of the numbers and usage of guns across the country. The Second Amendment was created only to protect the security of the country and to ensure the success of a "well-regulated militia". The amendment was not created to give all people the rights to use a gun.

Just as there are organizations to ensure that no gun control laws are passed, there are organizations that are lobbying Congress to enact gun control legislation. Among these are the Coalition to Stop Gun Violence, the Center to Prevent Handgun Violence, and Handgun Control, Inc.

Although their names are similar, these organizations have very different goals. For example, the Coalition to Stop Gun Violence, a very liberal organization, believes that all handguns should be banned from all citizens, and should only be used by military and police forces. As for those who use their guns for hunting, they would only be allowed to keep their guns if they were kept under lock and key at a gun club.

On the other hand, Handgun Control, Inc., supports a ban on the manufacturing and selling of a cheap gun known as the Saturday Night Special. They are also calling for an in-depth background check and an extended waiting period. They also favor extended jail time for the illegal use of guns, mandatory training for gun usage, greater responsibility on gun owners to keep their handguns secure, and to report missing firearms to the police.

The Center to Prevent Handgun Violence believes that guns such as the Saturday Night Specials are produced for criminals, not for the military or sportsmen. They want the manufacturers of these weapons to be responsible for the damage done with their weapons when it gets into the wrong hands.

Many people are lobbying for a national system of gun registration and licensing. Others want to increase the age requirement for people to own or use a gun. Also, it is suggested that gun owners must be tested on their knowledge of proper and safe firearm use, and must also be subject to getting re-licensed on a regular basis.

Advocates for gun control say that despite the fact that many families own a gun and feel that it is safe, the opposite is true. In fact, families who own a gun and only have it for security purposes have a greater chance of killing a family member than an intruder.

These facts were supported by studies reported in the New England Journal of Medicine. The Journal reported that for every justifiable homicide in the home, there are 1.3 accidental deaths, 4.6 unjustified homicides, and 37 suicides. The Journal also reported that guns are a small source of protection in a home, since 90 percent of all crimes that take place in the home occur when there is no one home.

As we take another look at the wording of the Second Amendment, we see that there is no mention of a permissive use for firearms when used for hunting or sport. Furthermore, prior to the drafting of the Second Amendment, there was no talk about the use of firearms for any purpose besides military force. Gun control advocates take this to mean that there is no legal right for anyone who is not part of a military force to own a gun.

In response to the argument that gun rights should certainly be protected for hunters, there have been many incidents that gun control advocates point to that indicates quite the contrary is true.

On February 13, 2006, Vice President Dick Cheney, an experienced hunter, went hunting with friends on a Texas ranch. While hunting for quail, the Vice President accidentally shot his hunting companion, Harry Whittington, in the face and chest. Fortunately, Whittington survived, even after suffering a heart attack immediately after the shooting.

This incident proved to America and the world that even hunters as experienced and careful as the Vice President can end up shooting people, rather than animals. The right to hunt, therefore, cannot be an exclusive, separate right from gun ownership in general; the risks posed to other people are the same as those posed by gun owners who do not use their weapons to hunt.

The American Medical Association (AMA) has published many studies on gun-related deaths. One of those studies found that gun-related deaths are the second highest killer of high-school-age people. In order to reduce the number of gun-related deaths, the AMA has introduced new initiatives to restrict the amount of guns available. Examples of these restrictions are tests, licenses, and long waiting periods.

In 1939, the Supreme Court ruled on the Second Amendment, in a case known as U.S. v. Miller. In that

case, Arkansas bootlegger Jack Miller was indicted for
violating the National Firearms Act of 1934 by carrying a
sawed-off shotgun across state lines. Miller argued that the
case should be dismissed, since the Second Amendment
allowed him to carry the gun.

In that case, the Supreme Court ruled against Miller, saying that his shotgun had no "reasonable relationship to the
preservation . . . of a well-regulated militia" and was thus
not protected under the Second Amendment. It was also
noted that the weapon that was carried was not a normal
weapon, and its use "would not contribute to the common
defense."

It was recognized, however, that an individual had the
right to own a gun, but it must serve a collective purpose. The court also defined the term militia as a "body of
citizens enrolled for military discipline"- not as an armed
citizenry at large.

Subsequent to the ruling in *U.S. v. Miller*, many courts
have ruled that federal rulings regulating the use of firearms do not violate the Second Amendment unless the rulings interfere with the militia. Additionally, in later court
decisions, no court has ever ruled that individual rights to
own firearms are protected by the Second Amendment.

Many advocates for gun control believe that owning handguns should be illegal. Since there is no known use of
handguns in any militia, these weapons are considered by
many to be unprotected by the Second Amendment, and
therefore private ownership of these weapons is illegal.

When the Second Amendment had been drafted, the use
of firearms was necessary for the security of the colonies.

The militias were those responsible for the well being of those colonies. Later in time, however, these militias became known as the National Guard. Weapons of the National Guard are stored and dispersed by the state, and can be distributed quickly and safely during times of emergency.

As for those who believe the Second Amendment allows for gun ownership only by militias, there should be no barriers to strict gun control laws. This is because there are no more militias today. Therefore, they argue, private ownership of weapons is not protected under the law.

Therefore, if one day the states decide to reinforce and recreate a militia, they will successfully be able to hand out weapons to all their members under the law, without any federal interference.

When examining other countries around the world, evidence shows that there are far fewer gun-related deaths in almost all other counties combined than there are in America. This is because their governments do not have restrictions on the creation of strict gun control laws. This enables them to act swiftly and sensibly to create responsible gun control measures. If America can set an example to the rest of the world time and again by demonstrating the success of our democracy and our willingness to change, certainly this country can take an example from the rest of the world, and follow their successful approach to gun control to create a safer, better life for all Americans.

GUN CONTROL LAWS

It is approximated that there are more than 200 million guns in circulation today. With those numbers constantly increasing, the government must take a stand, and create laws that would limit the number of guns in circulation. Gun control is not a recent initiative. Gun control legislation was passed initially in the early 1900's. The laws created helped little, but helped. That is why we must do more. As the number of guns in circulation rise, so must the number of laws.

In the beginning of the twentieth century, the federal government began to realize that gun ownership and misuse was on the rise. They saw this as a potential for great loss, and an increase in crime. It was the 1920's - the period known as the Prohibition Era, when alcohol was declared illegal by the federal government. The Mafia had taken over the alcohol business, and just as in today's age we have drug trafficking, at that time, there was alcohol trafficking.

As this happened, many other mafia families saw the sale of alcohol as a great way to make a profit. They tried to kill off the other families, so that they could gain control of the alcohol business. At times, people in cities would watch as the gangsters fought with guns on the street for control of the lucrative business.

In 1927, Congress passed the Mailing of Firearms Act. This law prohibited all but certain people from sending "concealable" weapons through the postal system. However, this did not include the military, police, and arms manufacturers or legitimate gun sellers.

In the 1930's, the Great Depression had put millions of people out of jobs, and out of homes. Banks had closed down, and farms were deserted. Just as any time when the economy fails, the only successful enterprise is crime. Gangsters such as "Machine Gun" Kelly wandered the Midwest. As they traveled across the country armed with pistols, sawed-off shotguns, and rifles, they committed murder, robbed banks and businesses, and kidnapped the rich in return for ransom.

In 1934, Congress passed the National Firearms Act. This law required gun manufacturers to pay a heavy tax to the federal government when they made or sold machine guns, rifles, shotguns, and other firearms. This law was posed to manufacturers to discourage the production of guns by creating a large tax.

Then in 1938, another gun control law was enacted. It was called the Federal Firearms Act. This law required that manufacturers and sellers keep records of the guns they sold. This included registering the name of the purchaser, and the serial number of the weapon purchased. Criminals were forbidden to purchase guns, as were people under indictment.

The most comprehensive piece of legislation ever created was the Gun Control Act of 1968. Its enactment stemmed from the period of turmoil the country was in; the Civil Rights protests occasionally turned violent, as did the protests against the Vietnam War. It also emanated from national tragedies, such as the use of guns in the assassinations of John F. Kennedy, his brother, Robert, and civil rights leader Martin Luther King, Jr. (The latter two had occurred in 1968, the year Congress created the Gun Control Act).

This act, unlike the previous ones, was aimed at the choice of guns that criminals used. For example, it prohibited the use of Saturday Night Specials in the United States. It also prohibited the shipping of those guns to the United States. Previously, foreign nations made a big profit from selling these guns to the United States.

Also banned under the Gun Control Act of 1968 are:

- All weapons that can be concealed. This does not apply to guns such as pistols and revolvers. It is aimed at Saturday Night Specials, and guns which look like pens, known as "pen" guns.

- Shotguns manufactured with barrels under 18 inches in length.

- Machine guns.

- Rifles with barrels shorter than 16 inches.

- Any weapon resulting from a shortening of a shotgun to an overall length of 26 inches, or any rifle cut to 26 inches.

- Any silencers or machines used to lower the sound a gun makes when fired.

- Major devices. Included here are the bazooka, cannons, rockets, or dangerous explosives.

- Restricts interstate purchasing. This means that you cannot buy a gun in one state, and bring it over to your home in another state. Under this law, people who buy guns in one state and live in different states must have their guns transferred to a dealer in their state.

There are also limits on the ages of people who can buy guns. To buy a long gun, you must be 18 years old, and to buy a handgun, you must be 21 years old. At the time of its creation, the Gun Control Act was the most comprehensive Gun Control Act ever. It promised to bring an end to the use of guns for illegal purposes, but did allow the use of guns for sporting purposes.

The Gun Control Act was missing something, however. Despite the fact that it did not allow the importation of cheap handguns, it did allow for the importation of parts. This upset many gun control advocates, because once the parts were shipped to the United States, they could be assembled and sold there.

In 1979, another piece of gun legislation emerged from Congress. That year, Congress had passed the Firearm Owners Protection Act. This act was a bipartisan bill introduced to Congress by Republican Idaho Senator James McClure, and Missouri Democratic Representative Harold Volkmer. This law allowed interstate gun sales to go forth, as long as the laws of the state of the seller, and the laws of the state of the buyer were not violated. The part of the Act that pleased gun control advocates was that background checks would continue.

As the years since 1979 passed, Senator McClure and Representative Volkmer had passed amendments for the Gun Control Act. One of those amendments set requirements for gun sellers and manufacturers. President Ronald Reagan signed the Act in 1986.

As the years went on, violence in the public schools had increased. It had become almost unbearable for some, and some students began staying home from school out of fear of being shot. So the Congressional enactment of the Gun-Free School Zones Act of 1990 was a godsend to those who suffered with the thoughts of going to school, and never coming back alive.

The Gun-Free School Zones Act made it a federal offense to have guns within the area of a school. The National Education Association (NEA) wanted the passage of a stricter gun control law, the Violence-Free School Bill. This bill would supply $100 million annually for five years to schools for tighter security. With this money, schools would buy metal detectors, train teachers for ways to deal with violence in schools, and create other security initiatives.

On March 30, 1981, President Ronald Reagan was walking to his limousine after delivering a short speech to the AFL-CIO. A spectator named John W. Hinckley dropped to one knee, and used a .22-calibur Roehm RG14 revolver to shoot at President Reagan. He fired six shots, and struck Reagan in the left lung. Reagan was then transported to

George Washington University Hospital, where he underwent surgery. He recovered in a few weeks.

His press secretary, however, was not as fortunate. James Brady was shot on the right side of his brain and suffered severely. Miraculously he survived, but the massive injuries had left his left side completely injured. He also lost his capability of short-term memory, and had a slurred speech. Even today, he has problems with mundane things, such as eating, and getting out of bed.

The severity of what had happened left the country and it's leaders in shock. Congress decided to make another piece of gun control legislation. The result of many discussions and debates on the floor of the Congress was the Brady Handgun Violence Prevention Act.

The Brady Bill, as it is commonly referred to, was simple. It required that all people must wait five days before receiving a gun after an application to purchase one is made. Before this bill, only some states had laws pertaining to a waiting-period.

During the waiting period, law enforcement officials would check the gun buyer's background. They would check if the man was a felon, an alcoholic, mentally unstable, e.t.c. They would also check the prospective buyers criminal record to see if he had infringed on any laws in the past. The law, however, does not make it absolutely necessary for enforcement officials to complete the background check; rather, they do so at their own will. They have a choice whether to search the background of the prospective buyer, or not. If they feel that the prospective buyer is a law-abiding citizen, they can waive the background check on that person at their own discretion.

The waiting period served another purpose as well. Besides the background checks, it allowed for a cooling off period for the prospective buyer. If a man wanted to purchase a gun to kill someone at the spur of the moment, he would have to wait a certain number of days before getting his gun. During that time, he would have an opportunity to think about whether he actually wants to kill that person or not.

For example, when John Hinckley shot President Reagan, he used a gun that he had very recently purchased. Gun control advocates argue that had there been stricter gun control laws, such as the Brady Bill, John Hinckley would never have been able to purchase the gun, and fire at President Reagan. (Of course, prior to the attempted assassination of President Reagan, there was no such gun control initiative proposed like the Brady Bill, rather, gun control advocates argued that the enactment of the Brady Bill would prevent future incidents such as the one that happened to James Brady).

Under the proposed act, a gun dealer had to obtain the prospective buyer's name and address, and obtain a document with the buyer's picture on it (a document such as a driver's license would do just fine). The customer then has to give the dealer a document stating that he or she is not prohibited under law from obtaining a firearm. That document is then given to a local law enforcement officer. At the end of the waiting period, if the dealer receives word that the buyer's record is clear, the dealer may then proceed with giving the buyer his or her gun. The dealer may not supply the buyer with a firearm if he or she receives word that the buyer's record is not completely clear of infringements.

Under this act, a gun buyer may have their waiting period waived if they can prove that their life is in some way being threatened. Also, if the buyer has a gun permit he or she received within the last five years, the waiting period may also be waived.

The background check introduced by the Brady Bill requires an extensive check of the buyer's background. This includes checking the federal record as well. Under the Brady Bill, any prospective buyer who has had run-ins with the law in the past would be prohibited from purchasing a gun.

Not surprisingly, the NRA strongly opposed the Brady Bill. The NRA's director of national affairs, James J. Baker, told the House Judiciary Subcommittee on Crime and Criminal Justice that the Brady Bill restricts the rights of people to purchase guns. He also said that the claim that John Hinckley would never have been able to do what he did had he been subject to a background check is invalid. He claimed that since John Hinckley did not have a criminal record, he would have been allowed to purchase the gun at the time he did.

Then U.S. Representative Charles Schumer spoke in favor of the Brady Bill. He said, that during the Persian Gulf War, "Our first mission . . . was to take the weapons away from the Iraqi enemy; our first mission at home must be to take the guns away from our criminals . . ." He did say however, that enacting the Brady Bill would not take away the crime; it would mitigate it.

In a vote of 239 to 186 in the House of Representatives, the Brady Bill was passed by recommendation from the House Judiciary Subcommittee. The bill then went on to the Senate, where it was passed into law. However, it did not become the law, because the two houses disagreed on additions to the legislation, and the Brady Bill stalled.

In 1984, Congress passed the Armed Career Criminal Act, which gave tougher penalties to criminals who possessed guns. The law said that if one had three convictions for burglary or robbery, and had a gun when they committed another crime, their minimum prison sentence would be extended from 10 to 15 years, and possibly be as much as life imprisonment without parole.

A Gallup Poll conducted between March 12 and 14, 1993, showed that Americans overwhelmingly supported gun control legislation. Of the 1,007 adults who were polled, 88 percent supported the bill, 67 percent favored a bill that would limit people to buying one gun a month, and 66 percent supported a ban on semiautomatic assault weapons, which need very little reloading, and allow for more shots to be fired in a smaller span of time than a regular weapon.

In 1993, the Brady Bill was reintroduced to Congress. President Bill Clinton supported the bill. On February 17, 1993, he told Congress, "I'll make you this bargain: If you pass the Brady Bill, I'll sign it." Sure enough, Congress passed the Brady Bill, which enacted into law a five-day waiting period before a pistol was given to a buyer, at which time a background check would be made of that person's record.

True to his word, President Bill Clinton signed the Brady Bill into law, in the last weeks of 1993.

Below is a survey produced by Handgun Control, Inc. It has data collected from 22 law enforcement agencies in 15 states. The data is the total number of Brady Checks conducted in 1995, as well as all the denials for gun ownership based on background checks:

DEPARTMENT	NUMBER OF BRADY CHECKS	DENIALS
Arizona Department of Public Safety	88,668	2,229
Arkansas State Police Department	28,298	537
Colorado Department of Public Safety	52,894	3,373
Idaho Department of Law Enforcement	28,633	883
Kentucky State Police	59,500	1,129
Nevada Highway Patrol	31,067	552
S. Carolina Law Enforcement Department	53,157	2,106
Utah Department of Public Safety	33,314	560
West Virginia State Police	25,288	187
Albuquerque (NM) Police Department	4,521	163

DEPARTMENT	NUMBER OF BRADY CHECKS	DENIALS
Amarillo (TX) Police Department	2,532	52
Choctaw (OK) Police Department	85	1
Corpus Christi (TX) Police Department	3,218	166
Dallas (TX) Police Department	12,994	921
El Paso (TX) Police Department	4,774	220
New Orleans (LA) Police Department	11,237	1,124
Oklahoma City (OK) Police Department	14,130	252
Plano (TX) Police Department	2,093	52
San Antonio (TX) Police Department	10,122	210
Shawnee County (KS) Sheriff's Department	1,877	77
Total	468,402	14,794

Different states have different ways of handling the issue of guns. Twenty-three states have no gun legislation at all. Below are examples of the efforts of some states to prevent the loss of life to gun violence.

In California, there is a fifteen-day waiting period and mandatory background checks for gun purchases. Since 1991, California has banned the sale of AR-15s, AK-47s, and dozens of other military firearms. Residents of California must register any military firearms they own, such as, Uzis, AR-15s, AK-47s, and all semiautomatic weapons. There are harsh fines for violating this law, such as $350 for the first offense, and jail time for further violations.

According to the state, there are very few Californians who obey the law. There are estimates that there are 300,000 guns that need to be registered under the law, yet there are only 5,150 of them who have been registered. The fifteen-day waiting period, however, has proven to be advantageous. In 1992, for example, the following have been prevented from purchasing guns:

- 71 people convicted of homicide.

- 14 people convicted of kidnapping.

- 141 people who have been put on restraining orders for domestic violence.

- 884 people convicted of robbery.

- 1,283 people convicted of drug offenses.

- 5,772 people convicted of assault.

In 1992, a school bus in the city of New Haven was caught in the crossfire of gangs. In the shoot-out, a kindergarten student was shot in the head. Responding to the incident, Governor Lowell P. Weicker called Connecticut's legislature in to discuss the enactment of gun control legislation.

After several debates, the legislature agreed on several gun control bills.

One required an individual to be eighteen years old to purchase a firearm. Also, it prohibited weapons to be brought within 1,500 feet of a school. This excluded law enforcement officials.

In Texas, there are no gun control laws. Therefore, there are many people who die from gunshot wounds. There are thousands of gun dealers throughout the state, and around 250 gun shows each year. When the incident at Waco occurred on February 28, 1993, four federal agents and six cultists had been killed by gunshots. It was reported that the Branch Davidians had many illegal machine guns. Ironically, most of these were created from legal parts.

In May of 1993, the Texas State Legislature had authorized a vote on whether it should be legal to carry a handgun. Governor Ann Richards had vetoed the bill because it would have cost the taxpayers 60,000 dollars to conduct a poll that could have been done by private pollsters.

The state of Virginia has a reputation of being a major gun dealer to states throughout the Northeast. A bill was passed to limit the purchase of guns to once a month. Their reputation, however, lives on. The ATF (Bureau of Alcohol, Tobacco, and Firearms) reported that one third of the guns seized in New York City and approximately one quarter of the guns seized in Washington, D.C. came from nowhere else but the state of Virginia.

In the aftermath of the September 11th, 2001 attacks, the United States recognized its vulnerabilities in the area of Homeland Security. One of the most important lessons that 9/11 taught the United States was the need to prevent, at all costs, terrorist organizations from strengthening their hold in the U.S. and abroad. Time and again it was mentioned that one of the ways to prevent future terrorist attacks was to ensure that dangerous weapons did not end up in the hands of potential terrorists.

The effort to restrict and destroy terrorist organizations was focused on groups outside the United States, but missed the overt terrorist cells operating inside the country. The need for weapons restrictions was obvious, yet no attempt was made to do so.

Earlier, in 1994, President Bill Clinton signed a ban on assault weapons into law. The law banned 19 types of military-style weapons whose primary use was for destruction on a massive scale. The ban stated, however, that the bill would be in effect for 10 years, at which point Congress needed to reauthorize it to extend it beyond its initial 10-year term.

In November 2000, a member of Hezbollah was arrested after a nine-month investigation by the FBI's counter-terrorism unit. Ali Boumelhem was convicted on seven counts of weapons charges and conspiracy to ship weapons and ammunition to Lebanon. Boumelhem, a resident of Detroit and Beirut, traveled to Michigan gun shows and bought gun parts and ammunition for shipment overseas. Boumelhem, a convicted felon, was prohibited from legally purchasing guns at gun stores. Boumelhem was convicted on September 10, 2001, and his charges stemmed from violating none other than the assault weapons ban.

This event highlighted different loopholes with the gun control laws. Background checks are required by gun shows, but only for federally licensed dealers, not private ones. Another problem is that the background checks only search for convicted criminals, but not for suspected ones. Potential terrorists who have never committed crimes, but may be on an FBI watch list, can easily get away with buying a gun.

When the United States military entered Afghanistan, they found an Al Qaeda manual entitled, "How Can I Train Myself for Jihad" in a training camp. In this manual, was a section on "Firearms Training" for would-be terrorists. The manual specifically mentioned the United States for its easy availability of firearms, and said that al-Qaeda members living in the United States could "obtain an assault weapon legally, preferably AK-47 or variations."

In 2004, at the height of the presidential campaign, Congress refused to extend the assault weapons bill, despite the obvious need for it. Threats of future terrorist attacks, coupled with the pre-existing need for tighter gun control laws, did nothing to sway the Congress to ensure that the ban would remain in place. As a result, terrorists and criminals were allowed to purchase these weapons, making American cities and communities more vulnerable to large-scale terrorist attacks.

It is finally time for Congress and the President to address this growing problem in America. The NRA sees gun ownership as a right, and gun control as a barrier placed on one's legal right to own a gun. But when you think about it, is that correct? The NRA speaks of gun control as unconstitutional, and a violation of all the rights this country was founded upon. But what about the lives of ordinary Americans? What about the lives of the people who live in fear of getting shot? Aren't their rights being violated as well?

What about the right to live without the fear of dying? What about the fact that students who go to school today are living in fear of their own classmates, their own friends, and neighbors?

We need to think about the police officers that are killed in the line of duty protecting the common welfare of this country. What about America, the nation that declared its independence from tyranny and harsh rule? What has happened since? The Founding Fathers would never have dreamed of America turning into the gun show of the world.

Today, this country has more gun-related deaths than any country in the world. Do you think our Founding Fathers wanted that? Do you think they envisioned America the way it is today?

America declared its independence on July 4, 1776. They declared that they wanted to be separated from Great Britain. In the Declaration of Independence, they outlined the reasons for the necessity of Independence. Tyranny, harmful leadership, and harsh laws had caused a country to declare its independence. The people who founded America ran away from fear. However, today we live in fear. It is time to declare our independence from these fears, and create a better America.

FAMOUS COURT DECISIONS

Supreme Court Cases

U.S. v. Cruikshank (1876)

This decision was the first Second Amendment case to reach the Supreme Court. This case involved members of the Ku Klux Klan who burned down a Louisiana courthouse that was occupied by a group of armed blacks. They were accused of denying their black victims their basic civil rights as stated in the First and Second Amendments of the Constitution, such as freedom of assembly and the right to bear arms. The court decided that the federal government had no power to correct these violations, and the citizens had to rely on the states for their protection from private individuals.

The decision read, "The right of the people peaceably to assemble for lawful purposes existed long before the adoption of the Constitution of the United States." The court ruled, therefore, that these rights weren't created by the Constitution; they were natural rights, in place before the Constitution was written. The power to enforce them existed with the states, not with the federal government. Therefore, individuals could not file charges against other citizens in federal court regarding violations of their constitutional rights.

Presser v. People of Illinois (1886)

Presser v. Illinois involved Herman Presser, who was found guilty of leading an assembly of armed men without authorization in Illinois. Presser charged that the Illinois law violated the Second Amendment. The Court ruled the states have the power to control and regulate military bodies, including drilling and parading activities. The Court re-affirmed the *Cruikshank* decision of 10 years before, by saying that the Second Amendment was a limitation on the federal government.

However the Court also wrote that despite the fact that the rights of enforcement belong to the States, they couldn't deny people the right "from keeping and bearing arms". The reason, they said, was because the States did not have the rights "to deprive the United States of their rightful resource for maintaining the public security"; i.e., the right of the federal government to have militias.

Miller v. Texas (1894)

This case dealt with Franklin Miller, a shoemaker who lived with a black slave and her mullato child in Texas. Racial tensions at the time ran high, and accusations were made that he was having a personal relationship with the maid as well. The police and others continually harassed him, until a shootout erupted one morning between him and police officers, after the officers attempted to arrest him for violating a Texas law that forbade people from carrying weapons unless they had "reasonable grounds for fearing an unlawful attack". Witnesses offered conflicting testimony about exactly what happened, but at the end of the shootout, Miller had killed a police officer.

Miller was later convicted of murder, and appealed his case. He claimed that his Second and Fourth Amendment rights were violated, but the Court dismissed his claim, in part because he had not made that claim in his original trial. Additionally, the Court said that his rights were not violated, because the Texas law was legal. The decision essentially reaffirmed *Cruikshank*, by saying that the States have the authority to control laws governing gun use. Once again, the Court ruled that the federal government was restricted by the Second Amendment, and had no power over the States abilities to legislate on that issue.

U.S. v. Miller (1939)

Jack Miller and Frank Layton were charged with violating the 1934 National Firearms Act, which required registration and taxation of different weapons. The decision the Court rendered here was that the National Firearms Act did not step over the boundaries of the federal government's limits on regulating gun use, as prescribed in the *Cruikshank* decision and reaffirmed in *Presser* and *Miller*.

The Court ruled that "it is not within judicial notice that a shotgun having a barrel of less than 18 inches in length is any part of the ordinary military equipment or that its use could contribute to the common defense." Therefore, they ruled, the Act, which made the sawed-off shotgun illegal, was Constitutional by virtue of the fact that militias did not use such a weapon. As a result, the National Firearms Act did not violate the Second Amendment, which only gave gun ownership rights to those who used guns that could be used for the common defense.

The Court also discussed at length the meaning of the term "militia". They said, "The Militia comprised all males physically capable of acting in concert for the common defense." Essentially, the Court ruled that all such people could legally own weapons, since they could contribute to the national defense. Along with this reasoning, any weapons that could be used in a militia were permitted; any weapons which did not, i.e., the weapon in question in this particular case, can certainly be prohibited.

Lewis v. U.S. (1980)

This is the final case the Supreme Court has heard that directly affected the interpretation of the Second Amendment. In this case, Lewis was a convicted felon who was prevented from legally owning a gun. He claimed that his conviction was the result of his failure to have a counsel present at his trial. He was charged with illegally owning a gun in violation of the law.

The Court argued that his conviction for illegal possession of the weapon was a fair one; as there were "remedies available to a convicted felon" by which he could have had consent to legally own the firearm. For this reason, the Court decided, Congress did not violate the Constitution by prohibiting felons from owning weapons.

Additionally, since felons cannot vote or practice medicine, it is Constitutional to prevent them from owning guns as well. This can also be a logical conclusion based on the fact that the government is meant to protect the citizens of its nation- putting a weapon in the hands of a convicted criminal would endanger the public, and therefore should logically be illegal.

Lower Court Cases

U.S. v. Tot (1942)

Frank Tot was charged with violating the National Firearms Act by taking possession of a weapon after he had been charged with a crime. Tot claimed that if the law banning weapons included the weapon he had, the law must be unconstitutional. The court ruled that Tot failed to show that there was a connection between his weapon and the preservation of a militia. This requirement was outlined in the *Miller* decision three years before. Since there was no evidence that Tot used it for militia purposes, he was not protected under the Second Amendment.

Cases v. United States (1942)

Jose Cases Velazquez transported a .38 Caliber Colt type gun and ammunition in Puerto Rico in violation of the Federal Firearms Act. The weapon he transported was known to be a military-style weapon, and Cases did not belong to any military. He challenged the constitutionality of the Act, but his claims were dismissed.

The court ruled that Congress has the power to legislate over the territories as well, and therefore the Act had jurisdiction in Puerto Rico. The decision also stated that the *Miller* decision did not make a general rule about which guns were protected by the Second Amendment and which ones were not. Therefore, in this decision, the court ruled that there were many weapons that were not protected.

U.S. v. Decker (1971)

Audry Decker was charged for failing to make the proper entries and maintain records when selling a firearm as required by the 1968 law. In this case, federal agents used a false name to contact Decker to buy guns from him. When they bought the guns, Decker did not make any record of the sale, and was charged. In court, Decker claimed entrapment by the agents, but the court ruled that there was no entrapment because the agents never suggested that records not be kept. He appealed, but the conviction stood.

The relevant claim that Decker made was that the 1968 Gun Control Act was unconstitutional because it lacked certain specificity. The court ruled that Decker's claim that the Act was vague was unreasonable. The reason, they said, was because the Act did meet the criteria of a law that can be easily understood. That criteria, they said, was "to give a person of ordinary intelligence fair notice that his contemplated conduct is forbidden by the statute."

Decker also challenged the Act's constitutionality, saying it violated his Second Amendment rights. The decision of the court quoted the *Miller* decision, and said that because his violation did not contribute to a militia, the Second Amendment did not safeguard his actions.

U.S. v. Cody (1972)

James Cody illegally made false statements to a firearms dealer when he was buying a gun. He was asked to sign a paper stating that he had not been convicted of a crime punishable by more than a year in prison. He signed it, but later claimed he was unaware of that stipulation. Cody had previously been convicted of a crime that was punishable by 5 years in prison. By lying to the licensed gun dealer, he committed a crime.

He appealed his conviction, saying that the law was unconstitutional. The Appeals Court upheld the conviction, saying the law did not violate the Second Amendment. Furthermore, they ruled that Congress was in their right to pass such a law, since it was legal under the Commerce Clause of the Constitution for the Congress to regulate even intrastate gun trading, since the dealer was federally licensed.

U.S. v. Swinton (1975)

Charles Swinton was a known gun dealer who sold guns without a license. He met many times with undercover federal agents who attempted to buy guns from him. They had little success at first, but finally, he did sell them some. He was charged for selling guns without a license, but claimed the law only applied to those whose primary occupation was that of a gun dealer.

The court dismissed that claim, saying that his behavior indicated that he was a gun dealer, and his definition of a gun dealer was not accurate under the law. They reiterated the definition of dealer as, "any person engaged in the business of selling firearms wholesale or retail".

U.S. v. Oakes (1977)

Ted Oakes had owned an unregistered machine gun in Kansas City, Kansas. The Kansas City Police had taken the gun away, welded the barrel shut, and then returned the gun to Oakes. An undercover agent met with Oakes numerous times in his house, and bought several guns from him. One of these guns was the machine gun that had been welded shut. Before Oakes sold the gun, he had opened the barrel, and with a few minor adjustments, the weapon would have been a fully functional machine gun.

Oakes' relevant claim was that the law violated his Second Amendment right allowing him to own guns. He claimed that as a member of "Posse Comitatus", he was a member of a militia, and therefore had a constitutional right to own the machine gun. The court ruled that "Posse Comitatus" was not a governmental militia, and therefore his rights were not protected under the Second Amendment.

Quilici v. Village of Morton Grove (1982)

In 1981, the Village of Morton Grove, Illinois, passed an ordinance banning most types of handguns. This ordinance followed an uproar caused by the proposed opening of a gun shop near a school in the Village. The ordinance was challenged, and came before the United States Court of Appeals, which affirmed the decision of a lower court to uphold the ordinance. The challenge to the ordinance was manifold, but the pertinent challenge was Quilici's contention that the ordinance violated the Second Amendment.

Quilici argued that the ordinance did affect the public welfare, since the people would not be able to arm themselves in self-defense. The court found their argument to be without merit, arguing that Quilici's argument "offer[ed] no authority, other than their own opinions, to support their arguments". Their claim that the ordinance was unconstitutional on the basis of other Amendments was also dismissed.

U.S. v. Nelsen (1988)

In 1982, Congress passed the Switchblade Knife Act, which prohibited any transportation, sale, or use of switchblades. Douglas John Nelsen believed that this law was unconstitutional, and began importing foreign-made switchblades, which were mailed to his home and post office box and distributed through his own business. Nelsen was indicted for violating the Act, and appealed his case to the Eight District Circuit Court of Appeals.

One of his many claims arguing the unconstitutionality of the Act was that it violated the Second Amendment. The Court cited the Supreme Court decisions in *Miller*, *Cruikshank*, and other major decisions, stating that the Second Amendment only protects the militia. In this case, the court ruled that the Act did not harm any militia, and therefore was constitutional.

U.S. v. Emerson (1999, 2001)

On October 20, 1997, Dr. Timothy Emerson, of San Angelo, Texas, purchased a 9mm Beretta. Approximately one year later, on August 28, 1998, Dr. Emerson's wife, Sacha, filed a petition for divorce in state district court for Tom Green County, Texas. On September 4, 1998, the Judge held a hearing for entry of "Temporary Orders," as is standard practice in Texas. Around that time, Dr. Emerson called his wife, and threatened to kill a friend of hers.

On December 8, 1998, a Federal Grand Jury indicted Dr. Emerson for violation of a law that prohibited possession of a firearm or ammunition while there is a particular type of injunction in effect. Dr. Emerson's attorney moved to overturn the indictment, and the U.S. District Court dismissed the indictment as violating the Fifth Amendment and the Second Amendment rights of Dr. Emerson. The government appealed to the Fifth Circuit.

Emerson claimed the charges against him violated his Fifth Amendment rights because possession of the gun was a "valuable liberty interest", which is protected under the Fifth Amendment. The District Court agreed with him, but the 5th Circuit Court moved to overturn the District Court's dismissal of Dr. Emerson's indictment for many reasons. Since he made a credible threat over the phone to his wife, he was not protected under the law. Additionally, when he purchased the weapon, he signed BATF Form 4473, which said that if he were under a court order he would no longer be allowed to possess the weapon.

Another claim Emerson levied against the charges made against him was that the law violated his Second

Amendment rights as well. The District Court found that
the law was unconstitutional on those grounds, since the
law was a state law that interfered with a federal law;
namely, the Second Amendment right to own guns. Since
the law did not allow one who was undergoing divorce
proceedings to own a gun, even if that person (like
Emerson), committed no crime, the law was inherently
unconstitutional.

The Fifth Circuit Court, in their 2001 decision, over-
turned the dismissal of the indictments, and of the Second
Amendment, said that the District Court was right in ruling that the Second Amendment protected citizens' rights
to own weapons, however those rights could be limited.
In this case, the Circuit Court ruled that Emerson was
enough of a threat to warrant the suspension of his Second
Amendment rights to possess a weapon. The case then
went to a trial that lasted only one day. After the trial,
Dr. Emerson was convicted of possessing the Beretta, and
was sentenced to thirty months in a federal penitentiary.

PART V:

PREVENTING VIOLENCE

Risk Factors

According to the federal government's Office of Juvenile Justice and Delinquency Prevention, in 1995, 84 percent of all counties in the United States had no juvenile homicides, and 10 percent of the counties reported only one. Additionally, 25 percent of all known juvenile homicides that year were committed in five cities: Chicago, New York, Los Angeles, Detroit and Houston. Together, these cities only contain about 10 percent of the nation's population, yet they comprise 25 percent of all known juvenile homicides.

One of the reasons all those murders took place in those cities was the development of gangs. In Chicago, psychologist Robert Zager and his colleagues went to work on this issue. What they published was astounding. The researchers found that a boy's chances of committing murder are twice as high if he has the following risk factors: (Note: These factors will be discussed in-depth later in this chapter.)

- His family has a history of repeated criminal violence.

- He has a history of being abused.

- He drinks alcohol or uses drugs.

- He is a member of a gang.

It was also found that his odds triple when in addition to the factors mentioned above, the following also occurs:

- He has been arrested.

- He currently owns or uses a weapon.

- He has academic difficulties at school.

As these and many other risk factors accrue in a child, he or she has a greater risk of killing someone. It is rarely the case that one single risk factor can definitively prove whether the child is capable of murder. Rather, it is the buildup of many risk factors that account for the actions they will take in the future.

In the beginning of this chapter, five cities were mentioned as the concentrated areas of the country where juvenile homicides occur. These are Chicago, Los Angeles, New York, Detroit and Houston. These cities contain areas where many children are exposed to many of the risk factors that were discussed. These areas are neighborhoods where there are the highest rates of adult criminality, gang activity, drug use, illicit drug sales, child abuse, school failure, abundant use of handguns, knives, and other dangerous weapons. In addition, these cities, especially New York and Chicago, have experienced extreme racial discrimination. It has been long recognized that the experience of racial discrimination provokes feelings of rage, and incites violent reactions as well.

It is also interesting to note that many United States citizens are most affected by their historical background. For example, all the states in the South that were members of the Confederacy during the Civil War were on the list of the twenty states with the highest homicide rates. The ten states with the lowest rates were located in New England and the northern Midwest. In 1996, Louisiana's homicide rate was around twelve times that of South Dakota.

Historian Roger Lane states in his book "Murder In America", that in the 1960's, America's big cities had murder rates that were lower than the national average, because states in the South had the highest rates. One connection between Southern culture and violence is that it reflects the system of slavery and the violence associated with the Civil War.

It is also noted that in the South, public religion plays an important role in the violence there. Religions legitimize violence as a means to obtain revenge, and some even feel compelled to act out violently. It is also the history that is passed from generation to generation that account for the homicides there.

The risk factors that were researched by Dr. Robert Zager and those that were discussed earlier, are increasing:

- Child Abuse: According to the National Incidence Study by the U.S. Department of Health and Human Services, from 1986 to 1993, the rate of child abuse increased from 14 per 100,000 to 23 per 100,000. These figures represent only children who have experienced harm. Those at risk for harm grew even greater, from 22 per 100,000 to 42 per 100,000.

- More recent data suggests that there are almost 1,000,000 confirmed cases of child abuse a year. However, it is believed that most incidents of child abuse go unreported, and so it is likely that the figures surpass 2,000,000 incidents a year. The numbers of reported incidents are irrelevant, as child abuse statistics are now recorded as incidents that meet the definition of child abuse, as dictated by the 1996 Federal Child Abuse Prevention and Treatment Act.

- Substance Abuse: Drugs have spread across the United States. Almost every community has drugs. The Center for Disease Control and Prevention reported that 9 percent of all high-school-age males had used cocaine. Also, 50 percent of adolescent males reported having used marijuana, and 30 percent had used it in the previous month. From 1976 to 1994, there has been an overall decrease in the use of drugs among teens. Since 1994, the overall rate has increased. Every year, about 10% of people aged 12-17 abuses a drug of some sort. At this time, methamphetamines have rapidly become the drug of choice- not only for teens, but working adults as well.

- Alcohol Abuse: Heavy alcohol use among teenagers is all too common: In 2004, the Department of Health and Human Services reported that about 18% of 12-17 year olds abused alcohol. Alcohol is also widely believed to cause upwards of 100,000 deaths a year as a result of drunk driving, and physical ailments caused by alcohol.

- Gangs: According to the federal government, the formation of youth gangs is on the rise in communities across America. According to recent surveys, more and more children are reporting that there are active gangs in their school and community. It is believed that from 1989 to 1995 gang activity has risen 50 percent, and has not fallen significantly since then.

- Weapons: There is an increase in the likelihood that kids will carry weapons. Many do so because they feel unprotected and threatened, and that adults can't help them. Fascination with guns, when started at a young age, can lead to horrible consequences. Such was the case of Andrew Golden of Arkansas, and Kip Kinkel of Oregon, as well as many other students who brought guns to school, and killed many people with them. Many of those spent hours immersed in the study of guns.

- Arrests: Since 1980, youth arrests have increased dramatically - up 50 percent from 1980 to 1994. Also, many police officers have taken a different approach to arresting teens - they take them home, instead of jail. They also talk to the offender's parents, and do not involve the legal system in the child's indiscretions. The trend for youth arrests over the last 10 years shows a decline in the number of youth arrests, but there are still too many incidents to dismiss it as a cause for violence.

- Difficulties in School: For every thirty-day period, one in three high school students report having skipped school for at least one day. Research also reveals that increasing rates of behavioral, emotional, and intellectual problems affect the ability to succeed in school. Since 1969, the percentages of students who have cheated on tests have risen from 34 percent to 68 percent. According to the Center for Disease Control, in 1997, 20 percent of all high school-age-boys reported that they were in a physical fight on school property in the past year, and 26 percent said that their property had been severely damaged or stolen on school property. Four percent of high school boys said that in the previous month, they felt too unsafe to go to school on at least one occasion.

The continuing rise in statistics relating to all factors that contribute to gun violence in schools, communities, or any other places, will not stop by itself. Legislative action must be taken to the extent that it can to prevent a further rise in contributing factors. By doing so, the likelihood of any future gun violence will be seriously diminished. By attacking the root of the problem; i.e., the causes which lead to further violence, we can stem the tide of gun violence in the future.

METHODS OF PREVENTION

Violence is rampant all over America. This book is meant to focus on the violence in our school system. Many organizations specialize in creating awareness programs about violence, and offering ways to help prevent future violence. This chapter deals specifically with those initiatives.

To reduce violence on campus:

- A local school committee should be established by school districts. Planning and creating safety measures and regular review of security measures should be implemented.

- Send rules of conduct home to be read by students and parents/guardians. Require students and parents/guardians to sign and return a form of agreement to the rules to the school. Hold regular meetings to communicate rules to parents/guardians, and inculcate such ideas into regular PTA meetings.

- A comprehensive crisis management plan should be developed by schools to help students and staffers act rationally when faced with a calamity.

- Updates on safety plans and training should be done regularly to keep the school and its staff informed. The training should include classified staff, regular staff, and all members of the school.

- Community volunteers, including parents, should be used to help patrol neighborhoods surrounding the school a few hours before and after school, as well as all hours that the school is open.

- Establish a relationship with local law enforcement and nearby businesses and establishments that allow for wide-ranging monitoring of student activity during school hours.

- Encourage all residents and passersby near the school to report any misconduct. Establish a system within the school to handle calls from the neighborhood.

- All points of possible entry should be monitored. Entry points should be as limited as possible. All access points should be monitored by campus security, and video cameras should be installed as well.

- All visitors should be required to sign in and out, and all deliveries should be monitored closely.

- Students should be taught to report individuals who may seem suspicious, or activity which appears suspicious. They should also learn safety techniques, and resolutions to conflicts.

- A special class should be instituted that focuses on teaching students techniques that deal with nonviolence, conflict-resolution, and appropriate ways to handle difficult situations that require quick but effective decisions.

- Alternative schools should be established that are fully equipped to handle students who cannot function properly with normal students. There must be other schools set up for these children, in order to keep them off the streets, and prevent further violence.

Methods to prevent greater consequences of school violence:

- Emergency drills should be held often to familiarize the exact actions students should take in a time of crisis. This has been proven to work. For example, in Cleveland Elementary School in Stockton, California, a man carrying an AK-47 opened fire on the school playground. In less than five minutes, five children were dead, the gunman was dead, and 29 other students were injured, 15 seriously. Before the shooting, school officials held frequent emergency drills. When the shooting occurred in their school, there was no hysterical behavior from the children. They followed directions from the adults, and the shooting, although one of the deadliest ever, could have been worse had the emergency drills not been held.

- The school must maintain their campus, and keep the grounds clean and clear. This will prevent anyone from being able to hide anywhere on school property.

- Emergency telephones should be installed outside the school, in the parking lot, and on all the fields. This will allow anyone who sees something suspicious to report it right away.

- Offer a reward to all those who inform school officials about any guns on the campus. By offering a monetary award, or any other incentive, students will inform the authorities of guns and other dangerous weapons. The confidentiality of the student informer is kept, and further crises are avoided.

Communications

Communication to students, law enforcement, staff, and parents is crucial during a time of emergency. Here are some suggestions that could help communication, and decrease panic in a time of a crisis:

- Designate at least one unlisted telephone line for use during an emergency.

- Always have a portable telephone readily available in case of an emergency. It is also useful when the phone lines are down.

- An emergency communication set should be assembled, and should consist of emergency telephone numbers, a phone book, a fax machine, and an Internet connection. Equipment such as this is found in almost all schools today.

- Telephone recording equipment, although not an absolutely necessary item, should be connected to the phone lines in case a bomb threat is made.

- Two-way radios as well as CB's should be used to communicate with personnel in times of emergency.

Bullying prevention:

- Assess the bullying problem in the school by talking to students and staff, and discuss ways to prevent bullying.

- Discuss clear standards for behavior with students. Outline for them what kind of behavior is expected, and what kind is not acceptable.

- Staff and teachers should always be within seeing range on campus. Ensure that all students are aware of your presence, so that disaster is avoided.

- Staff and teachers should always be monitoring playgrounds and hallways, or any place in the school building that is infamous, and known to be a center of fights.

- Warn or suspend offenders of school policies on bullying. If problem persists, cases should be referred to school psychologists.

- Provide counseling for bullies. Public or private, these discussions will help. Offer students incentives to cooperate with the rules, and make sure that they understand the penalty if they do not.

Teacher's guide to identifying victims of bullying:

- School staff should be aware that victims of bullying are generally younger, smaller, and weaker than the bullies.

- Staffers should take all bullying incidents to the highest authority possible.

- Teachers should be attentive to symptoms of bullying. Victims may experience a drop in grades, or be afraid or hesitant to go to school. If a child is missing for a period, become suspicious, and find out why.

- Teachers should encourage children to talk about events in the student's life, such as activities the student engages in after school. This could have broader effects on creating a safer school in regards to other areas, such as alcohol or substance abuse.

There are many other things that a teacher or staffer can do to help prevent violence in our schools. It is the first step towards making our schools a safer place for everyone.

Conclusion

Throughout the writing of this book, it has become increasingly obvious that the problem of gun violence in America is very grave. No one can imagine how extensive this problem really is. It is a problem that has dug itself right into the very core of this country. It has far surpassed anyone's imagination, and to deal with this problem we require great strength, purpose, and resolve.

This book has given an extensive look at the entire issue of gun violence in America. This issue clearly begs for the reforms necessary to make our nation safe again. To see the children of our nation dying is not something any one of us can tolerate any further. We cannot send children to schools thinking they are safe, and today, the students themselves cannot go to school and feel safe.

There are many children whom we may or may not know. We may see them every day; we may think that he or she is the smartest student, or the most popular one. However, we do not know what the child does in their private moments. We do not know if the child has access to guns, or whether he uses them or even has used them.

History has taught us that often times, when children use weapons; their problem is simply an emotional one. Whatever the problem is, one thing is certain. Without a gun, he or she can kill no one. People can also help this student by offering them counseling. He or she, after talking to someone, will not resort to the violent means they otherwise might have. Everything does not have to end in violence; there is a simpler solution.

The importance of passing legislation on all levels of government to reform this issue cannot be underestimated. Our shared responsibility as citizens of this great nation must compel citizen and legislator alike to action. Many options are available, and the time is ripe to act on them.

We must first move to enforce the laws we have in effect today. By empowering more government agencies to track down and prosecute those who violate these laws, more criminals will be taken off the streets, and our communities will be safer.

We also need to focus on closing the loopholes in our current laws. Laws with loopholes that allow terrorists to purchase weapons at gun shows are not laws we should continue to tout as successful. Many of our laws are archaic; they fail to protect Americans in today's world, and they are inefficient at combating the current threat of gun violence in America.

We must continue to fight for new gun control legislation. The ban on assault weapons must be reinstituted, and it must be made permanent as well. New laws restricting gun ownership must also be passed, and the waiting period for background checks done on prospective gun buyers must be extended as well.

Proposals made advocating a national gun registry deserve thoughtful debate. Careful consideration must also be given to all proposals limiting access to guns in our nation, for we never know which new law will save lives- the lives of our friends and family may hang in the balance.

What we really must focus on is limiting the access of guns to children in America. If we can successfully eradicate the presence of guns in the lives of young people across our nation, we will be far more likely to live in a more secure nation for generations to come. By disarming our youth, we can ensure long-term success in the fight against crime and violence in America.

Lao-Tzu once said, "A journey of a thousand miles must begin with a single step." On the issue of controlling gun violence in America, many steps must be taken before we reach a point of security. However, we must take that single step; if for nothing else, than to save our children.

APPENDIX

ORGANIZATIONS TO CONTACT

Center For The Study And Prevention Of Violence
University of Colorado at Boulder
439 UCB
Boulder, CO 80309
(303) 492-8465

This organization is headed by Dr. Delbert Elliot. The center is located in the University of Colorado, and has researched "what works" in the area of violence prevention programs. They compile research and offer aid for developing violence prevention programs.

The Brady Center To Prevent Gun Violence
1125 I Street N.W., Suite 1100
Washington, D.C. 20005
(202) 289-7319

This organization helps to create awareness about the risks of owning a handgun. It sponsors programs for high-school students that include discussions about the role of the handgun in society, and causes and methods of preventing handgun violence. It supports stronger regulation of the gun industry, but opposes a ban on all weapons. They employ grassroots efforts and fundraising to promote their agenda.

The Brady Campaign To Prevent Gun Violence
1225 I Street N.W., Suite 1100
Washington, D.C. 20005
(202) 898-0792

This organization is a public citizens lobby working for legislative controls and governmental regulation of every aspect of the gun trade, including the manufacture, sale, and distribution of firearms. It compiles statistics, research reports, and other informational data on firearms. It also publishes books and newsletters, and presents awards to those associated with the issue. This organization was founded by Handgun Control, Inc., which changed its name to its current one in June, 2001.

Educational Fund To End Handgun Violence
110 Maryland Avenue N.E.
Washington, D.C. 20002
(202) 544-7227

This organization works alongside other organizations interested in controlling gun violence. It deals with educating people about matters related to handgun violence, and is fighting for tougher background checks and supports closing loopholes in gun laws. It helps develop educational programs for schools in an effort to persuade children not to carry guns. It deals with automatic-weapons violence, and conducts research and compiles statistics as well. This organization is also known as the Coalition to Stop Gun Violence.

Mediascope
12711 Ventura Boulevard, Suite 440
Studio City, CA 91604
(818) 508-2080

This organization works to create awareness about the way the media affects society. It encourages responsible depictions of social and health issues in films and articles. It has produced many publications, including "How Children Process Television", and the "National Television Violence Study."

National Crime Prevention Council
1000 Connecticut Avenue, N.W., Thirteenth Floor
Washington, D.C. 20036
(202) 466-6272

This organization provides training and assistance to those interested in crime prevention. It advocates recreational programs as a means to reduce youth violence. It also consults with various organizations and governments, educating them about crime preventions. It sponsors the "Take A Bite Out Of Crime" campaign, and publishes the newsletter "Catalyst" 10 times a year.

National Institute of Justice
National Criminal Justice Reference Service
P.O. Box 6000
Rockville, MD 20849
(800) 851-3420
(301) 519-5500

This organization is affiliated with the U.S. Department of Justice, and supports research on crime, crime prevention, and criminal behavior. The National Criminal Justice Reference Service is a storehouse for criminal justice information for researchers and individuals.

National School Safety Center
141 Duesenberg Drive, Suite 11
Westlake Village, CA 91362
(805) 373-9977

This organization studies school crime and violence, including hate crimes. Their main purpose is to create an awareness of the problems that disrupt education, and offer ways to solve those problems. They provide training, assistance, legal aid, and publications for their cause. They develop strategies that make school safety a part of the academic curriculum to ensure that safety is a top priority. They publish their newsletter "School Safety Update" nine times a year.

Office of Juvenile Justice & Delinquency Prevention
810 Seventh Street N.W.

Washington, D.C. 20531
(202) 307-5911

This organization is the primary federal agency charged with monitoring and improving the juvenile justice system. Among its many goals is the prevention of crime and drug use by juveniles. They work to rehabilitate delinquents and give them the treatment they need. They distribute fact sheets and reports dealing with juvenile delinquency.

Partners Against Violence Network Online
www.pavnet.org
(301) 504-5462

This organization is a virtual library of information about youth violence, and has data from several federal agencies. It promotes the prevention of youth violence through education as well as through recreation. It offers a plethora of information on community, family, and youth violence, as well as substance abuse. It also provides information about prevention and rehabilitation for victims and abusers alike. It provides links to government agencies as well as nonprofit organizations involved in similar issues. Its monthly newsletter, "PAVNET Online", is also available.

Prevent Violence On Your Campus
2455 Teller Road
Thousand Oaks, CA 91320
(805) 499-9774

This organization provides training packets for principals, school officers, and teachers. The producers of these packets know that violence is a major concern, and inform people of ways to deal with such violence. These packets present "at-risk" students with information on how to better their future by presenting positive alternatives for them to choose from.

Violence Prevention Curriculum For Adolescents
EDC Publishing Center
555 Chapel Street, Suite 24
Newton, MA 02160
(800) 225-4276

This organization addresses the growing rates of violence and homicide among children. It alerts students to the risks of being involved in an act of violence, and offers alternatives to violence, such as anger management. This curriculum has proven to be effective as a means of preventing violence.

BIBLIOGRAPHY

Books

Anderson, Jack. <u>Inside The NRA: Armed And Dangerous</u>. Los Angeles, CA: Dove Books, 1996.

Baldick, Robert. <u>The Duel: A History of Duelling</u>. London: Chapman And Hall, LTD: 1965

Behr, Edward. <u>Prohibition: Thirteen Years That Changed America</u>. New York: Arcade Publishing, 1996.

Bellesiles, Michael. <u>Arming America: The Origins Of A National Gun Culture</u>. New York: Alfred A. Knopf, 2000.

Bode, Janet and Stanley Mack. <u>Hard Time: A Real Look At Juvenile Crime And Violence</u>. New York: Delacorte Press, 1996.

Bok, Sissela. <u>Mayhem: Violence As Public Entertainment</u>. Reading, MA: Perseus Publishing, 1999.

Bruce John M. and Clyde Wilcox, eds. <u>The Changing Politics Of Gun Control</u>. Lanham, MD: Rowman and Littlefield, 1998.

Carter, Gregg Lee. <u>The Gun Control Movement</u>. New York: Twayne Publishers, 1997.

Cox, Vic. <u>Guns, Violence, And Teens</u>. Springfield, NJ: Enslow, 1997.

Crooker, Constance E. <u>Gun Control And Gun Rights</u>. Westport, CT. Greenwood Press, 2003.

DeConde, Alexander. <u>Gun Violence In America</u>. Boston, MA: Northeaster University Press, 2001.

Diaz, Tom. <u>Making A Killing In America: The Business of Guns In America</u>. New York: The New Press, 1999.

Dolan, Edward F. and Margaret M. Scariano. <u>Guns In The United States</u>. Danbury, CT: Franklin Watts, 1994.

Garbarino, James. <u>Lost Boys</u>. New York: The Free Press, 1999.

Grapes, Bryan J. <u>Violent Children</u>. San Diego, CA: Greenhaven Press, 2000.

Helmer, William J. <u>The Gun That Made The Twenties Roar</u>. Highland Park, NJ: Gun Room Press, 1969.

Kruschke, Earl R. <u>Gun Control: A Reference Handbook</u>. Santa Barbara, CA: ABC-Clio Inc., 1995.

LaPierre, Wayne. <u>Guns, Crime and Freedom</u>. New York: Harper Perrenial, 1995.

McCullough, David. <u>1776</u>. New York: Simon & Schuster, 2005.

Robin, Gerald D. <u>Violent Crime And Gun Control</u>.
  Cincinnati, OH: Anderson Publishing, 1991.

Roleff, Tamara L. <u>Gun Control: Opposing Viewpoints</u>.
  San Diego, CA: Greenhaven Press, 1997.

Schneider, Dona. <u>American Childhood: Risks And
  Realities</u>. New Jersey: Rutgers University Press, 1995.

Sherrow, Victoria. <u>Violence And The Media: The
  Question Of Cause And Effect</u>. Riverside, NJ:
  Millbrook Press, 1996.

Spitzer, Robert J. <u>The Politics of Gun Control</u>. Chatham,
  New Jersey: Chatham House, 1995.

Strahinich, Helen. <u>Think About Guns In America</u>. New
  York: Walker & Co., 1992.

Tirman, John. <u>Spoils of War: The Human Cost of
  America's Arm Trade</u>. New York: Free Press, 1997.

Wheeler, Eugene S. and Anthony S. Baron. <u>Violence In
  Our Schools, Hospitals, And Public Places</u>. California:
  Pathfinder Publishing, 1993.

Zelnick, Bob. <u>Gore: A Political Life</u>. Washington, DC:
  Regnery Publishing, 1999.

Websites

American Psychological Association. <www.apa.org>

Americans For Gun Safety.
  <www.americansforgunsafety.com>

British Broadcasting Company. <www.bbc.co.uk>

Bureau of Alcohol, Tobacco, Firearms, and Expolsives.
  <www.atf.treas.gov>

CNN News. <www.cnn.com>

Dave Kopel Online. <www.davekopel.com>

Firearms And Liberty. <www.firearmsandliberty.com>

Frontiers Of Freedom. <www.opinioneditorials.com>

GunCite. <www.guncite.com>

Mediascope. <www.mediascope.org>

Mothers Against Videogame Addiction And Violence.
  <www.mavav.org>

National Education Association Health information
  Network. <www.neahin.org>

National Rifle Association. <www.nrahq.org>

National School Safety And Security Services.
  <www.schoolsecurity.org>

National School Safety Center. <www.schoolsafety.us>

Partnership Against Violence Network.
  <www.pavnet.org>

Sane Guns. <www.saneguns.org>

The Brady Center To Prevent Gun Violence.
  <www.bradycenter.org>

The International Association of Chiefs of Police.
  <www.theiacp.org>

United States Department of Health And Human
  Services. <www.hhs.gov>

United States Department of Justice. <www.usdoj.gov>

Violence Policy Center. <www.vpc.org>